THE
DHAMMAPADA

THE DHAMMAPADA

SAYINGS OF THE BUDDHA

THE ESSENTIAL WISDOM LIBRARY

TRANSLATED BY

F. MAX MÜLLER

ST. MARTIN'S
ESSENTIALS
NEW YORK

Published in the United States by St. Martin's Essentials,
an imprint of St. Martin's Publishing Group

Printed in the United States of America. For information, address
St. Martin's Publishing Group, 120 Broadway, New York, NY 10271.

www.stmartins.com

The Library of Congress Cataloging-in-Publication data is available upon request.

ISBN 978-1-250-85226-7 (trade paperback)
ISBN 978-1-250-85227-4 (ebook)

Our books may be purchased in bulk for promotional, educational, or business use.
Please contact your local bookseller or the Macmillan Corporate and Premium
Sales Department at 1-800-221-7945, extension 5442, or by email at
MacmillanSpecialMarkets@macmillan.com.

First St. Martin's Essentials Edition: 2022

10 9 8 7 6 5 4 3 2 1

This edition seeks to faithfully reproduce the original publications of the author's
works and so has maintained the original spelling and grammar throughout, with
only minor alterations for clarity or content.

Contents

Preface

IT has been a great and unexpected pleasure to me to have to bring out a new, the third edition of my translation of the Dhammapada. The first was published in 1870, the second in 1881. I cannot indeed pretend to have improved the present edition very much, for I have not had any time left during the last few years to continue my study of Pâli. Nor has Pâli ever been more than a *parergon* to me. I began it in 1845 during my stay at Paris with Burnouf, who was then almost the only scholar who could read Pâli texts, and I still have a letter of his in which he apologises for his imperfect knowledge of the language. At that time Pâli scholarship had not yet become a special and independent study, but it was a kind of annexe to Sanskrit. Men like Bopp and Burnouf were expected to teach not only Sanskrit and Comparative Philology, but at the same time, Zend, the Prâkrit dialects, and, as one of them, Pâli. Clough's Pâli Grammar (Colombo, 1824 and 1832) and Turnour's Mahâvanso (1837) were all that we had to depend on. Some advance was made by Spiegel and Westergaard, but the real impulse to an independent and scholarlike study of Pâli literature came from my friend Childers, the author of the first Pâli Dictionary, published in 1875. Before that time the only names to be mentioned in Pâli scholarship were those of James D'Alwis, Spence Hardy, Spiegel, E. Kuhn, Minayeff, Senart, Weber, and last, not least, Fausböll. After the publication of Childers' Dictionary, the progress of Pâli scholarship has been very rapid, and the number of Pâli texts and translations has increased very considerably. As the most active among the new generation of Pâli scholars deserve to be mentioned Rhys Davids, the founder of the Pâli Text Society, Oldenberg, the editor of the Vinaya-pitaka, Trenckner, E. Senart, Féer, Morris and the translators of the Gâtaka, Professor E. B. Cowell, Messrs. R. Chalmers, W. H. D. Rouse, H. T. Francis, and R. H. Neil.

The most favourite Pâli text seems to have been the Dhammapada. It is certainly a most interesting collection of verses, giving a trustworthy picture of Buddhist thought, particularly in its practical and moral character. Consisting of short sentences it seems at first an easy book to translate, but the very fact that these *versus memoriales* stand by themselves without any context to throw light on them creates a peculiar difficulty, much the same as that with which the readers of another elementary book, the Hitopadesa, are well acquainted. Like the Hitopadesa, the Dhammapada also may be called an easy and at the same time a very difficult book. The verses being often torn from the context to which they originally belonged, may indeed be rendered word by word, but they leave us often in the dark, particularly where two readings are possible, which of the two we ought to choose; while if we knew what preceded and followed them in their original context, we should find our choice much easier. Though many difficult and obscure passages in the Dhammapada have now by a succession of translators and commentators been elucidated, many more still remain which require renewed study. It may seem strange to outsiders that there should still be so much uncertainty as to the exact meaning of many Pâli words. The meaning of the very title of our book, the Dhammapada, is still contested. I have produced whatever arguments I could collect in support of the meaning of 'Path of Virtue' or 'Path of the Law.' But I am far from saying that the translation 'Collection of Texts of the Law,' 'Worte der Wahrheit,' is impossible. What we want to settle the point is some ancient Buddhist authority to tell us with what intention this title was originally given. For titles are often fanciful, and mere scholarship is not sufficient to enable us to speak with magisterial assurance.

Let us take another instance. One of the commonest words in Buddhist philosophy is saṅkhâro. It corresponds to Sanskrit saṃskâra. The meanings of the Sanskrit word are difficult enough. It means the forming of matter, it can mean refining, polishing, embellishing, also the preparing of food and the moulding of clay Purifying rites also are called saṃskâra and the impressions of the mind as well as the result of them, the dispositions, tastes, talents or inclinations, may go by the same name. In Pâli, however, the growth of the meanings of saṅkhâro becomes far more complicated. It means there also preparing, but the Buddhist, as if remembering that saṃskâra meant etymologically putting together, and then what has been put together, uses saṅkhâro in the sense of anything that has been made and will therefore perish. According to Hindu philosophy whatever has been put together or made can be put asunder or unmade, and thus saṅkhâro came to be used not only for what we should call the created or material world, but for anything in it that is anitya or perishable. Thus saṅkhâro may sometimes be rendered by matter in general, though chiefly by organised or living matter, except that saṅkhâro includes what we should call attributes also. Lastly, like saṃskâra, saṅkhâro may mean the impressions left on the mind, and the resulting states of the mind predispositions, talents or character, in which sense it is often used by the Sâṅkhya philosophers. If then we read v. 368 that the quiet place or Nirvâna is saṅkhârupasamam sukham or happiness arising from the quieting of the saṅkhâras, we may translate either 'from the cessation of all existing things,' or 'from the calming of all desires or affections.' Hence Fausböll translates 'naturarum sedatio;' Weber, 'wo aufhören die Einkleidungen;' Gray, 'life-ending;' Hu, 'où cessent les existences;' v. Schroeder, 'wo alles Ding zur Ruhe kommt,' whereas I prefer to take upasama in the sense of calming, and saṅkhâro in the sense of all states of the mind, more particularly the calming of all desires and affections.

If such a verse occurred in a text treating either of the end of the world and all created things or of the subduing of all affections or passions, we should know at once which meaning to choose, while in our case we may, I think, allow ourselves to be guided by the word sukha, happiness, which seems to point to the quieting of the affections of the mind rather than to the destruction of the world.

In looking at the literature devoted to the Dhammapada, we may read very clearly the steady progress of Pâli scholarship. Fausböll's edition of the text with a Latin translation, and with extracts from the native commentary, which was published in 1855, marked indeed an epoch, if we may use such a hackneyed expression of a work of real importance and permanent value. It was indeed a work *sui generis,* and there was no other scholar living at the time who would have ventured on such new ground as that chosen by that young Danish scholar. It ought never to be forgotten that the publication of an Oriental text never published before, and the translation of an Oriental text never translated before, requires a kind of scholarship quite different from that of the patient follower who is satisfied with *jurare in verba magistri*. There is between a scholar such as Fausböll and the ordinary scholars who can read what has been read and translated before, about the same difference as between a Stanley exploring the darkest Africa and a tourist who now goes to Egypt personally conducted by Messrs. Cook & Co. Naturally the pioneer is apt to lose his way and to make mistakes. These very mistakes, however, are sometimes most creditable, just as the bold adventures of those who did not discover the sources of the Nile have often required greater efforts and entailed more severe sufferings than the successful discoveries of later comers. But be that as it may, no true Pâli scholar will ever forget what we owe to Fausböll's adventurous daring, no one pointing out improvements in his text and translation would not feel ashamed to blame or to ridicule him. In that respect Pâli scholarship may indeed be proud for having always preserved the temper of the true Buddhist or the gentleman, and it seems almost as if the best Pâli scholars had been those who were most thoroughly imbued with the true spirit of Buddha himself, and to whom nothing seemed so offensive as *pharusham*, which—sit venia—one might almost translate by *langage farouche ou grossier.*

After the first editor and translator followed—but longo intervallo—those who for the first time translated the text into a new language, whether German, English or French. To this class belong the translations of Weber (German), myself (English), Hu (French). No one who has not himself tried to translate Oriental thought into any European language can have any idea of the almost impossible task of finding words in any of these modern languages exactly corresponding to the ancient terms of Eastern religion or philosophy. To find terms exactly corresponding to the varied terminology of Buddhism is simply impossible. They do not exist, as little as there are modern coins corresponding exactly to a kârshâpana. Here nothing remains but to use terms of more general meaning which at all events are not wrong, and which, though they do not exactly cover the Pâli terms, yet include them. This is the rule I have tried to follow throughout. It is not very satisfactory, but it is better at all events than to use a word which is actually wrong or covers but a small segment of the original term.

In some cases the native commentary is of great help, and scholars who formerly despised the help of native interpreters, such as Sâyana or Buddhaghosa, are now agreed that they form a *sine qua non* in a critical study of ancient texts. How, for instance, should we know the right meaning of such a verse as 353, where we read:

'I have conquered all, I know all, in all conditions of life I am free from taint; I have left all, and through the destruction of thirst I am free; having learnt myself, whom should I teach?'

It is true we know now, and might have known before, that Pâli uddis is not used in the sense of teaching, but means pointing towards a person or a thing. In Sanskrit also upadis means teaching (anweisen), but not uddis, which means to point to.

A very similar verse occurs in the Suttanipâta 210:

Sabbâbhibhum sabbavidum sumedham
Sabbesu dhammesu anupalittam
Sabbangaham tamhakkhaya vimuttam
Tam vâpi dhîrâ munim vedayanti,

which Fausböll translates: 'The man who has overcome everything, who knows everything, who is possessed of a good understanding, undefiled in all things (dhamma), abandoning all things, liberated in the destruction of desire (nibbâna), him the wise style a Muni.'

Here all traces of the event which gave rise to the utterance of the verse have disappeared. But the commentator tells us that it was uttered originally by Buddha when on his way to Benares he met an Upagîvaka who asked him who it was that ordained him, and who was the teacher whose doctrine he taught. It was then that Buddha declared that he could point to no one as his teacher, but that he was his own teacher. After this all becomes clear, and we see that the verb uddis is the right verb to use for pointing out. We have only to refer to the Lalita-vistara XXVI, to see the story of the native commentator confirmed. Here kasmin Gautama brahmakaryam ukyate corresponds to kam uddissa pabbagito, that is, who gave thee leave to become a bhikshu or a pabbagita?

I subjoin a list of books containing translations or notes on the Dhammapada, published after the publication of my own translation, so far as they have become known to me:

(1) Le Dhammapada, par Fernand Hu, Paris, 1878.
(2) The Dhammapadam or Scriptural Texts translated from Pâli on the basis of Burmese MSS., by James Gray, 1881; sec. ed. Calcutta, 1887.
(3) Das Dhammapadam, Ein Vers. sammlung, aus der Englischen Übersetzung von Professor M. M.: metrisch ins Deutsch übersetzt, Leipzig, 1885.
(4) Der Wahrheitsphad, übersetzt von K. E. Neumann, 1893.

(5) A translation from a Chinese translation of the Dham-
     mapada by Samuel Beal was published in 1878, and is
     useful sometimes by the subjoined narratives.

Difficult passages have been discussed not only by Childers in
his Dictionary and in his 'Notes on the Dhammapada,' but likewise
by Morris in his valuable contributions to the Journal of the Pâli
Text Society, by Kern in his Bijdrage tot de Verklaring van eenige
woorden in Pali-geschriften voorkomende (Verhandelingen der
Kon. Akademie van Wetenschappen, Amsterdam, 1886), and by
Fausböll in his Nogle Bemærkninger om enkelte vanskelige Pâli-
Ord i Jâtaka-Bogen, 1888.

I have also to thank Prof. Fausböll, as formerly Childers, for
help given me in my translation. What I said in my introduction
to my former edition, that 'I can claim for myself no more than
the name of a very humble gleaner in this field of Pâli literature,'
applies with equal truth to the new edition. I have gleaned whatever grains seemed to me valuable in these later publications, and
have consulted several of the translators whenever there seemed
to be some points left that required to be cleared up.

F. M. M.

Introduction

The Dhammapada, a Canonical Book

The Dhammapada forms part of the Pâli Buddhist canon, though its exact place varies according to different authorities, and we have not as yet a sufficient number of complete MSS. of the Tipiṭaka to help us to decide the question[1].

Those who divide that canon into three Piṭakas or baskets, the Vinaya-piṭaka, Sutta-piṭaka, and Abhidhamma-piṭaka, assign the Dhammapada to the Sutta-piṭaka. That Piṭaka consists of five Nikâyas: the Dîgha-nikâya, the Magghima-nikâya, the Saṃyutta-nikâya, the Aṅguttaranikâya, and the Khuddakanikâya. The fifth, or Khuddakanikâya, comprehends the following works: 1. Khuddakapâtha; 2. DHAMMAPADA; 3. Udâna; 4. Itivuttaka; 5. Suttanipâta; 6. Vimânavatthu; 7. Petavatthu; 8. Theragâthâ; 9. Therîgâthâ; 10. Gâtaka; 11. Niddesa; 12. Paṭisambhidâ; 13. Apadâna; 14. Buddhavaṃsa; 15. Kariyâ-piṭaka.

According to another division[2], however, the whole Buddhist canon consists of five Nikâyas: the Dîgha-nikâya, the Magghima-nikâya, the Samyutta-nikâya, the Aṅguttaranikâya, and the fifth, the Khuddaka-nikâya, which Khuddaka-nikâya is then made to comprehend the whole of the Vinaya (discipline) and Abhidhamma (metaphysics), together with the fifteen books beginning with the Khuddaka-pâtha.

The order of these fifteen books varies, and even, as it would seem, their number. The Dîghabhânaka school admits twelve books only, and assigns them all to the Abhidhamma, while the Magghimabhânakas admit fifteen books, and assign them to the Sutta-pitaka. The order of the fifteen books is: 1. Gâtaka [10]; 2. Mahâniddesa [11]; 3. Kullaniddesa [11]; 4. Patisambhidâmagga [12]; 5. Suttanipâta [5]; 6. DHAMMAPADA [2]; 7. Udâna [3]; 8. Itivuttaka [4]; 9.Vimânavatthu [6]; 10. Petavatthu [7]; 11.Theragâthâ [8]; 12.Therîgâthâ [9]; 13. Kariyâpitaka [15]; 14.Apadâna [13]; 15. Buddhavamsa [14][3].

The Khuddaka-pâtha is left out in the second list, and the number is brought to fifteen by dividing Niddesa into Mahâniddesa and Kulla-niddesa.

There is a commentary on the Dhammapada in Pâli, and supposed to be written by Buddhaghosa[4], in the first half of the fifth century A.D. In explaining the verses of the Dhammapada, the commentator gives for every or nearly every verse a parable to illustrate its meaning, which is likewise believed to have been uttered by Buddha in his intercourse with his disciples, or in preaching to the multitudes that came to hear him.

Date of the Dhammapada

The only means of fixing the date of the Dhammapada is trying to ascertain the date of the Buddhist canon of which it forms a part, or the date of Buddhaghosa, who wrote a commentary on it. This, however, is by no means easy, and the evidence on which we have to rely is such that we must not be surprised if those who are accustomed to test historical and chronological evidence in Greece and Rome, decline to be convinced by it. As a general rule, I quite agree that we cannot be too sceptical in assigning a date to ancient books, particularly if we intend to use them as documents for tracing the history of human thought. To the initiated, I mean to those who have themselves worked in the mines of ancient Oriental literature, such extreme scepticism may often seem unscientific and uncalled for. They are more or less aware of hundreds of arguments, each by itself, it may be, of small weight, but all combined proving irresistible. They are conscious, too, of having been constantly on the look out for danger, and, as all has gone on smoothly, they feel sure that, in the main, they are on the right road. Still it is always useful to be as incredulous as possible, particularly against oneself, and to have before our eyes critics who will not yield one inch beyond what they are forced to yield by the strongest pressure of facts.

The age of our MSS. of the canonical books, either in Pâli or Sanskrit, is of no help to us. All Indian MSS. are comparatively modern, and one who has probably handled more Indian MSS. than anybody else, Mr. A. Burnell, has lately expressed his conviction that 'no MS. written one thousand years ago is now existent in India, and that it is almost impossible to find one written five hundred years ago, for most MSS. which claim to be of that date

· 3 ·

are merely copies of old MSS. the dates of which are repeated by the copyists[5].' This applies, however, to MSS. only which are written in the ordinary Devanâgarî alphabet.

Nor is the language, whether Sanskrit or Pâli, a safe guide for fixing dates. Both languages continue to be written to our own time, and though there are some characteristic marks to distinguish more modern from more ancient Buddhist Sanskrit and Pâli, this branch of critical scholarship requires to be cultivated far more extensively and accurately before true scholars would venture to fix the date of a Sanskrit or Pâli text on the strength of linguistic evidence alone[6].

The Buddhists themselves have no difficulty in assigning a date to their sacred canon. They are told in that canon itself that it was settled at the First Council, or immediately after the death of Buddha, and they believe that it was afterwards handed down by means of oral tradition, or, according to other authorities, actually written down in books by order of Kâsyapa, the president of the First Council[7]. Buddhaghosa, a learned and in some respects a critical scholar, living in the beginning of the fifth century A.D., asserts that the canon which he had before him, was the same as that fixed by the First Council[8].

Several European students have adopted the same opinion, and, so far as I know, no argument has yet been advanced showing the impossibility of the native view, that some collection of Buddha's doctrines was made immediately after his death at Râgagaha, and that it was finally settled at what is called the Second Council, or the Council of Vesâlî. But what is not impossible is not therefore true, nor can anything be gained by appealing to later witnesses, such as, for instance, Hiouen Thsang, who travelled through India in the seventh century, and wrote down anything that he could learn, little concerned whether one statement tallied with the other or not[9]. He says that the Tipi*t*aka was written down on palm leaves by Kâ*s*yapa at the end of the First Council. But what can be the weight of such a witness, living more than a thousand years after the event, compared with that, for instance, of the Mahâva*m*sa, which dates from the fifth century of our era, and tells us in the account of Mahinda's missionary journey to Ceylon (241/318), that the son of Asoka had to spend three years in learning the Tipi*t*aka by heart from the mouth of a teacher[10]? No mention is then made of any books or MSS., when it would have been most natural to do so[11]. At a later time, during the reign of King Va*tt*agâmani[12] (88–76 B.C.), the same chronicle, the Mahâva*m*sa, tells us that 'the profoundly wise priests had theretofore orally (mukhapâ*then*a) perpetuated the Pâli of the Pi*t*akattaya and its A*tth*akathâ (commentary), but that at this period the priests, foreseeing the perdition of the people assembled, and in order that the religion might endure for ages, recorded the same in books (potthakesu likhâpayu*m*)[13].'

No one has yet questioned the dates of the Dîpava*m*sa, about 400 A.D., or of the first part of the Mahâva*m*sa, between 459–477 A.D., and though no doubt there is an interval of nearly 600 years between the composition of the Mahâva*m*sa and the recorded writing down of the Buddhist canon under Va*tt*agâmani, yet we must remember that the Ceylonese chronicles were confessedly founded on an older A*tth*akathâ preserved in the monasteries of the island, and representing an unbroken line of local tradition.

My own argument therefore, so long as the question was only whether we could assign a pre-Christian date to the Pâli Buddhist canon, has always been this. We have the commentaries on the Pâli canon translated from Sinhalese into Pâli, or actually composed, it may be, by Buddhaghosa. Buddhaghosa confessedly consulted various MSS., and gives various readings, just as any modern scholar might do. This was in the beginning of the fifth century A.D., and there is nothing improbable, though I would say no more, in supposing that some of the MSS., consulted by Buddhaghosa, dated from the first century B.C., when Vattagâmani ordered the sacred canon to be reduced to writing.

There is one other event with reference to the existence of the sacred canon in Ceylon, recorded in the Mahâvamsa, between the time of Buddhaghosa and Vattagâmani, viz. the translation of the Suttas from Pâli into the language of Ceylon, during the reign of Buddhadâsa, 339–368 A.D. If MSS. of that ancient translation still existed, they would, no doubt, be very useful for determining the exact state of the Pâli originals at that time[14]. But even without them there seems no reason to doubt that Buddhaghosa had before him old MSS. of the Pâli canon, and that these were in the main the same as those written down at the time of Vattagâmani.

Buddhaghosa's Age

The whole of this argument, however, rested on the supposition that Buddhaghosa's date in the beginning of the fifth century A.D. was beyond the reach of reasonable doubt. 'His age,' I had ventured to say in the Preface to Buddhaghosha's Parables (1870), 'can be fixed with greater accuracy than most dates in the literary history of India.' But soon after, one of our most celebrated Pâli scholars, the great Russian traveller, Professor Joh. Minayeff, expressed in the Mélanges Asiatiques (13/25 April, 1871) the gravest doubts as to Buddhaghosa's age, and thus threw the whole Buddhist chronology, so far as it had then been accepted by all, or nearly all scholars, back into chaos. He gave as his chief reason that Buddhaghosa was not, as I supposed, the contemporary of Mahânâma, the author of the Mahâvamsa, but of another Mahânâma, the king of Ceylon.

Professor Minayeff is undoubtedly right in this, but I am not aware that I, or anybody else, had ever questioned so palpable a fact. There are certainly two Mahânâmas; one, the king who reigned from 410–432 A.D.; the other, the supposed author of the Mahâvamsa, the uncle and protector of King Dhâtusena, 459–477. 'Dhâtusena,' I had written, 'was the nephew of the historian Mahânâma, and owed the throne to the protection of his uncle. Dhâtusena was in fact the restorer of a national dynasty, and after having defeated the foreign usurpers (the Damilo dynasty) "he restored the religion which had been set aside by the foreigners"' (Mahâv. p. 256). Among his many pious acts it is particularly mentioned that he gave a thousand, and ordered the Dîpayamsa to be promulgated. As Mahânâma was the uncle of Dhâtusena, who reigned from 459–477, he may be considered as a trustworthy witness with regard to events that occurred between 410 and 432. Now the literary activity of Buddhaghosa in Ceylon falls in that period[15].'

These facts being admitted, it is surely not too great a stretch of probability to suppose, as I did, that a man whose nephew was king in 459–477, might have been alive in 410–432, that is to say, might have been a contemporary of Buddhaghosa. I did not commit myself to any further theories. The question whether Mahânâma, the uncle of Dhâtusena, was really the author of the Mahâvamsa, the question whether he wrote the second half of the 37th chapter of that work, or broke off his chronicle in the middle of that chapter, I did not discuss, having no new materials to bring forward beyond those on which Turnour and those who followed him had founded their conclusions, and which I had discussed in my History of Sanskrit Literature (1859), p. 267. All I said was, 'It is difficult to determine whether the 38th as well as the (whole of the) 37th chapter came from the pen of Mahânâma, for the Mahâvamsa was afterwards continued by different writers, even to the middle of the last century. But, taking into account all the circumstances of the case, it is most probable that Mahânâma carried on the history to his own time, to the death of Dhâtusena, 477 A.D.'

What I meant by 'all the circumstances of the case' might easily be understood by any one who had read Turnour's Preface to the Mahâvamsa. Turnour himself thought at first that Mahânâma's share in the Mahâvamsa ended with the year 301 A.D., and that the rest of the work, called the Sulu Wansé, was composed by subsequent writers[16]. Dharmakîrti is mentioned by name as having continued the work to the reign of Prâkrama Bâhu (A.D. 1266). But Turnour afterwards changed his mind[17]. Considering that the account of Mahâsena's reign, the first of the Seven Kings, terminates in the middle of a chapter, at verse 48, while the whole chapter is called the Sattarâgiko, 'the chapter of the Seven Kings,' he naturally supposed that the whole of that chapter, extending to the end of the reign of his nephew Dhâtusena, might be the work of Mahânâma, unless there were any strong proofs to the contrary. Such proofs, beyond the tradition of writers of the MSS., have not, as yet, been adduced[18].

But even if it could be proved that Mahânâma's own pen did not go beyond the 48th verse of the 37th chapter, the historical trustworthiness of the concluding portion of that chapter, containing the account of Buddhaghosa's literary activity, nay, even of the 38th chapter, would be little affected thereby. We know that both the Mahâvamsa and the somewhat earlier Dîpavamsa were founded on the Sinhalese Atthakathâs, the commentaries and chronicles preserved in the Mahâvihâra at Anurâdhapura. We also know that that Vihâra was demolished by Mahâsena, and deserted by nearly all its inmates for the space of nine years (p. 235), and again for the space of nine months (p. 237). We can well understand therefore why the older history, the Dîpavamsa, should end with the death of Mahâsena (died 302 A.D.), and why in the Mahâvamsa too there should have been a break at that date. But we must not forget that, during Mahânâma's life, the Mahâvihâra at Anurâdhapura was restored, that some kind of chronicle, called the Dîpavamsa, whether it be a general name of any 'chronicle of the island,' or of our Dîpavamsa, or, it may be, even of our Mahâvamsa, was ordered to be published or promulgated (dîpetum) under Dhâtusena, the nephew and protegé of Mahânâma. Therefore, even if we do not insist on the personal authorship of Mahânâma, we may certainly maintain that historical entries had been made in the chronicles of Anurâdhapura during Dhâtusena's reign, and probably under the personal auspices of Mahânâma, so that if we find afterwards, in the second half of the 37th chapter of his Mahâvamsa, an account of events which had happened between the destruction of the Mahâvihâra and the reign of Dhâtusena, and among them an account of so important an event as the arrival of Buddhaghosa from Magadha and his translation of the Sinhalese Atthakathâ into the language of Magadha, we may well suppose that they rest on the authority of native chronicles, written not long after the events, and that therefore, 'under all the circumstances of the case,' the age of Buddhaghosa can be fixed with greater accuracy than most dates in the literary history of India.

There is one difficulty still remaining with regard to the date of the historian Mahânâma which might have perplexed Turnour's mind, and has certainly proved a stumbling-block to myself. Turnour thought that the author of the commentary on the Mahâvamsa, the Vamsatthappakâsinî, was the same as the author of the Mahâvamsa, viz. Mahânâma. The date of that commentary, however, as we know now, must be fixed much later, for it speaks of a schism which took place in the year 601 A.D., during the reign of Agrabôdhi (also called Dhâtâpatisso). Turnour[19] looked upon that passage as a later interpolation, because he thought the evidence for the identity of the author and the commentator of the Mahâvamsa too strong to be set aside. He trusted chiefly to a passage in the commentary, and if that passage had been correctly rendered, the conclusion which he drew from it could hardly be resisted. We read in the Mahâvamsa (p. 254):

'Certain members of the Moriyan dynasty, dreading the power of the (usurper) Subho, the bâlattho, had settled in various parts of the country, concealing themselves. Among them there was a certain landed proprietor Dhâtusena, who had established himself at Nandivâpi. His son named Dhâtâ, who lived at the village Ambiliyâgo, had two sons, Dhâtusena and Sîlatissabodhi, of unexceptional descent. Their mother's brother (Mahânâma), devoted to the cause of religion, continued to reside (at Anurâdhapura) in his sacerdotal character, at the edifice built by the minister Dîghasandana. The youth Dhâtusena became a priest in his fraternity, and on a certain day, while he was chaunting at the foot of a tree, a shower of rain fell, and a Nâga, seeing him there, encircled him in his folds, and covered him and his book with his hood.... Causing an image of Mahâ Mahinda to be made, and conveying it to the edifice (Ambamâlaka) in which the thera's body had been burnt, in order that he might celebrate a great festival there, and that he might also promulgate the contents of the Dîpavaṃsa, distributing a thousand pieces, he caused it to be read aloud[20].'

If we compare with this extract from the Mahâvaṃsa a passage from the commentary as translated by Turnour, we can well understand how he arrived at the conclusion that it was written by the same person who wrote the Mahâvaṃsa.

Turnour translates (p. liv):

'Upon these data by me, the thera, who had, with due solemnity, been invested with the dignified title of Mahânâma, resident at the parivena founded by the minister Dîghasandana, endowed with the capacity requisite to record the narrative comprised in the Mahâvaṃsa, in due order, rejecting only the dialect in which the Singhalese Aṭṭhakathâ are written, but retaining their import and following their arrangement, the history, entitled the Palapadôruvaṃsa (Padyapadânuvaṃsa), is compiled. As even in times when the despotism of the ruler of the land, and the horrors arising from the inclemencies of the seasons, and when panics of epidemics and other visitations prevailed, this work escaped all injury; and moreover, as it serves to perpetuate the fame of the Buddhas, their disciples, and the Paché Buddhas of old, it is also worthy of bearing the title of Vaṃsatthappakâsinî.'

As the evidence of these two passages in support of the identity of the author and the commentator of the Mahâvaṃsa seemed to me very startling, I requested Mr. Rhys Davids to copy for me the passage of the commentary.

The passage runs as follows:

Yâ ettavatâ mahâvamsatthânusârakusalena Dîghasandasenâpat-inâ kârâpita-mahâparivenavâsinâ Mahânâmo ti garûhi gahi-tanâmadheyyena therena pubba-Sîhala-bhâsitâya Sîhalatthakathâya bhâsantaram eva vaggiya atthasâram eva gahetva tantinayânurûpena katassa imassa Padyapadânuvamsassa atthavannanâ mayâ. tam eva sannissitena âraddhâ, padesissariya-dubbutthibhaya-rogabhayâdi-vivi-dha-antarâya-yuttakâle pi anantarâyena nitthânam upagatâ, sâ buddha-buddhasâvaka-pakkekabuddhâdînam porânânam kik-kam pubbavamsatthappakâsanato ayam Vamsatthappakâsinî nâmâ ti dhâretabbâ. . . . Padyapadânuvamsavannanâ Vamsatthappakâsinî nitthitâ.

Mr. Rhys Davids translates this:

'The commentary on this Padyapadânuvamsa, which (latter work) was made (in the same order and arrangement, and re-taining the sense, but rejecting the dialect, of the Sinhalese com-mentary formerly expressed in the Sinhalese tongue) by the elder who bore the name of Mahânâma, which he had received from the venerable, who resided at the Mahâparivena built by the min-ister Dîghasanda, and who was well able to conform to the sense of the Mahâvamsa—(this commentary) which was undertaken by me out of devotion to that (history), and which (though thus undertaken) at a time full of danger of various kinds—such as the danger from disease, and the danger from drought, and the danger from the government of the province—has been safely brought to a conclusion—this (commentary), since it makes known the meaning of the history of old, the mission of the ancients, of the Buddhas, of their disciples, and of the Pakkeka Buddhas, should bear the name Vamsatthappakâsinî. . . .

'End of the Vamsatthappakâsinî, the commentary on the Padyapadânuvamsa.'

This shows clearly that Turnour made a mistake in translating this exceedingly involved, yet perfectly intelligible, passage, and that so far from proving that the author of the commentary was the same person as the author of the text[21], it proves the very contrary. Nay, I feel bound to add, that we might now argue that as the commentator must have lived later than 601 A.D., the fact that he too breaks off at verse 48 of chapter 37, seems to show that at his time also the Mahâvaṃsa did not extend as yet beyond that verse. But even then, the fact that with the restoration of the Mahâvihâra of Anurâdhapura an interest in historical studies revived in Ceylon, would clearly show that we may trust the date of Buddhaghosa, as fixed by the second part of the 37th chapter of the Mahâvaṃsa, at all events till stronger evidence is brought forward against such a date.

Now I am not aware of any such evidence[22]. On the contrary, making allowance for a difference of some ten or twenty years, all the evidence which we can gain from other quarters tends to confirm the date of Buddhaghosa[23]. I therefore feel no hesitation in here reprinting that story, as we find it in the Mahâvaṃsa, not free from legendary ingredients, it is true, yet resting, I believe, on a sound foundation of historical fact.

'A Brâhman youth, born in the neighbourhood of the terrace of the great Bo-tree (in Magadha), accomplished in the "viggâ" (knowledge) and "sippa" (art), who had achieved the knowledge of the three Vedas, and possessed great aptitude in attaining acquirements; indefatigable as a schismatic disputant, and himself a schismatic wanderer over Gambudîpa, established himself, in the character of a disputant, in a certain vihâra[24], and was in the habit of rehearsing, by night and by day with clasped hands, a discourse which he had learned, perfect in all its component parts, and sustained throughout in the same lofty strain. A certain Mahâthera, Revata, becoming acquainted with him there, and (saying to himself), "This individual is a person of profound knowledge, it will be worthy (of me) to convert him;" enquired, "Who is this who is braying like an ass?" The Brâhman replied to him, "Thou canst define, then, the meaning conveyed in the bray of asses." On the Thera rejoining, "I can define it;" he (the Brâhman) exhibited the extent of the knowledge he possessed. The Thera criticised each of his propositions, and pointed out in what respect they were fallacious. He who had been thus refuted, said. "Well, then, descend to thy own creed;" and he propounded to him a passage from the Abhidhamma (of the Piṭakattaya). He (the Brâhman) could not divine the signification of that passage, and enquired, "Whose manta is this?"—"It is Buddha's manta." On his exclaiming, "Impart it to me;" the Thera replied, "Enter the sacerdotal order." He who was desirous of acquiring the knowledge of the Piṭakattaya, subsequently coming to this conviction, "This is the sole road" (to salvation), became a convert to that faith. As he was as profound in his eloquence (ghosa) as Buddha himself, they conferred on him the appellation of Buddhaghosa (the voice of Buddha); and throughout the world he became as renowned as Buddha. Having there (in Gambudîpa) composed an original work called Ñânodaya (Rise of Knowledge), he, at the same time, wrote the chapter called Aṭṭhasâlinî, on the Dhammasangani (one of the commentaries on the Abhidhamma).

'Revata Thera then observing that he was desirous of undertaking the compilation of a general commentary on the Piṭakattaya, thus addressed him: "The text alone of the Piṭakattaya has been preserved in this land, the Aṭṭhakathâ are not extant here, nor is there any version to be found of the schisms (vâda) complete.

The Sinhalese Atthakathâ are genuine. They were composed in the Sinhalese language by the inspired and profoundly wise Mahinda, who had previously consulted the discourses (kathâmagga) of Buddha, authenticated at the three convocations, and the dissertations and arguments of Sâriputta and others, and they are extant among the Sinhalese. Preparing for this, and studying the same, translate them according to the rules of the grammar of the Mâgadhas. It will be an act conducive to the welfare of the whole world."

'Having been thus advised, this eminently wise personage rejoicing therein, departed from thence, and visited this island in the reign of this monarch (i.e. Mahânâma, 410–432). On reaching the Mahâvihâra (at Anurâdhapura), he entered the Mahâpadhâna hall, the most splendid of the apartments in the vihâra, and listened to the Sinhalese Atthakathâ, and the Theravâda, from the beginning to the end, propounded by the Thera Sanghapâla; and became thoroughly convinced that they conveyed the true meaning of the doctrines of the Lord of Dhamma. Thereupon paying reverential respect to the priesthood, he thus petitioned: "I am desirous of translating the Atthakathâ; give me access to all your books." The priesthood, for the purpose of testing his qualifications, gave only two gâthâs, saying, "Hence prove thy qualification; having satisfied ourselves on this point, we will then let thee have all our books." From these (taking these gâthâ for his text), and consulting the Pitakattaya, together with the Atthakathâ, and condensing them into an abridged form, he composed the work called the Visuddhimagga. Thereupon, having assembled the priesthood, who had acquired a thorough knowledge of the doctrines of Buddha, at the Bo-tree, he commenced to read out the work he had composed. The devatâs, in order that they might make his (Buddhaghosa's) gifts of wisdom celebrated among men, rendered that book invisible. He, however, for a second and third time recomposed it. When he was in the act of producing his book for the third time, for the purpose of propounding it, the devatâs restored the other two copies also. The assembled priests then read out the three books simultaneously. In those three versions there was no variation whatever from the orthodox Theravâdas in passages, in words, or in syllables. Thereupon, the priesthood rejoicing, again and again fervently shouted forth, saying, "Most assuredly this is Metteya (Buddha) himself," and made over to him the books in which the Pitakattaya were recorded, together with the Atthakathâ. Taking up his residence in the secluded Ganthâkara-vihâra (at Anurâdhapura), he translated, according to the grammatical rules of the Mâgadhas, which is the root of all languages, the whole of the Sinhalese Atthakathâ (into Pâli). This proved an achievement of the utmost consequence to all beings, whatever their language.

'All the Theras and Âkâriyas held this compilation in the same estimation as the text (of the Pitakattaya). Thereafter, the objects of his mission having been fulfilled, he returned to Gambudîpa, to worship at the Bo-tree (at Uruvelâya, or Uruvilvâ, in Magadha).'

Here[25] we have a simple account of Buddhaghosa[26] and his literary labours written by a man, himself a priest, and who may well have known Buddhaghosa during his stay in Ceylon. It is true that the statement of his writing the same book three times over without a single various reading, partakes a little of the miraculous; but we find similar legends mixed up with accounts of translations of other sacred books, and we cannot contend that writers who believed in such legends are therefore altogether unworthy to be believed as historical witnesses.

But although the date which we can assign to Buddhagho-sa's translation of the commentaries on the Pâli Tipitaka proves the existence of that canon, not only for the beginning of the fifth century of our era, but likewise, though it may be, with less stringency, for the first century before our era, the time of Vatt-agâmani, the question whether Buddhaghosa was merely a com-piler and translator of old commentaries and more particularly of the commentaries brought to Ceylon by Mahinda (241 B.C.), or whether he added anything of his own[27], requires to be more carefully examined. The Buddhists themselves have no difficulty on that point. They consider the Atthakathâs or commentaries as old as the canon itself. To us, such a supposition seems improba-ble, yet it has never been proved to be impossible. The Mahâvamsa tells us that Mahinda, the son of Asoka, who had become a priest, learnt the whole of the Buddhist canon, as it then was, in three years (p. 37)[28]; and that at the end of the Third Council he was despatched to Ceylon, in order to establish there the religion of Buddha (p. 71). The king of Ceylon, Devânampiya Tissa, was converted, and Buddhism soon became the dominant religion of the island. The Tipitaka and the Atthakathâ, such as they had been collected or settled at the Third Council in 242 B.C., were brought to Ceylon by Mahinda, who promulgated them orally, the Tipitaka in Pâli, the Atthakathâ in Sinhalese, together with an additional Atthakathâ of his own. It does not follow that Mahinda knew the whole of that enormous literature by heart, for, as he was supported by a number of priests, they may well have di-vided the different sections among them, following the example of Ânanda and Upâli at the First Council. The same applies to their disciples also. But the fact of their transmitting the sacred literature by oral tradition[29] was evidently quite familiar to the author of the Mahâvamsa. For when he comes to describe the reign of Vattagâmani (88–76 B.C.) he simply says: 'The profoundly wise priests had heretofore orally perpetuated the Pâli Pitakattaya and its Atthakathâ (commentaries). At this period these priests, foreseeing the perdition of the people (from the perversions of the true doctrines), assembled; and in order that the religion might endure for ages, wrote the same in books.' No valid objection has yet been advanced to our accepting Buddhaghosa's Atthakathâs as a translation and new redaction of the Atthakathâs which were reduced to writing under Vattagâmani[30], and these again as a translation of the old Atthakathâs brought to Ceylon by Mahinda[31]. There is prima facie evidence in favour of the truth of historical events vouched for by such works as the Dîpavamsa and the Mahâvamsa so far back at least as Mahinda, because we know that historical events were recorded in the monasteries of Ceylon long before Mahânâma's time. Beyond Mahinda we move in legendary history, and must be ready to surrender every name and every date as soon as rebutting evidence has been produced, but not till then.

I cannot, therefore, see any reason why we should not treat the verses of the Dhammapada, if not as the utterances of Buddha, at least as what were believed by the members of the Council under Asoka, in 242 B.C., to have been the utterances of the founder of their religion; nor can I see that even Professor Minayeff has shaken the date of Buddhaghosa and the general credibility of the Ceylonese tradition, that he was the translator and editor of commentaries which had existed in the island for many centuries, whether from the time of Vattagâmani or from the time of Mahinda.

Date of the Buddhist Canon

We now return to the question of the date of the Buddhist canon, which, as yet, we have only traced back to the first century before Christ, when it was reduced to writing in Ceylon under King Vattagâmani. The question is, how far beyond that date we may trace its existence in a collected form, or in the form of the three Pitakas or baskets. There may be, and we shall see that there is, some doubt as to the age of certain works, now incorporated in the Tipitaka. We are told, for instance, that some doubt attached to the canonicity of the Kariyâ-pitaka, the Apadâna, and the Buddhavamsa[32], and there is another book of the Abhidhammapitaka, the Kathâvatthu, which was reported to be the work of Tissa Moggaliputta, the president of the Third Council. Childers, s.v., stated that it was composed by the apostle Moggaliputta-tissa, and delivered by him at the Third Mahâsangîti. The same scholar, however, withdrew this opinion on p. 507 of his valuable Dictionary, where he says: 'It is a source of great regret to me that in my article on Kathâvatthuppakaranam I inadvertently followed James D'Alwis in the stupendous blunder of his assertion that the Kathâvatthu was added by Moggaliputtatissa' at the Third Convocation. The Kathâvatthu is one of the Abhidhamma books, mentioned by Buddhaghosa as having been rehearsed at the First Convocation, immediately after Gotama's death; and the passage in Mahâvamsa upon which D'Alwis rests his assertion is as follows, Kathâvatthuppakararanam paravâdappamaddanam abhâsi Tissatthero ka tasmim sangîtimandale, which simply means 'in that Convocation-assembly the Thera Tissa also recited (Buddha's) heresy-crushing Kathâvatthuppakarana.'

This mistake, for I quite agree with Childers that it was a mistake, becomes however less stupendous than at first sight it would appear, when we read the account given in the Dîpavaṃsa. Here the impression is easily conveyed that Moggaliputta was the author of the Kathâvatthu, and that he recited it for the first time at the Third Council. 'Wise Moggaliputta,' we read[33], 'the destroyer of the schismatic doctrines, firmly established the Theravâda, and held the Third Council. Having destroyed the different (heretical) doctrines, and subdued many shameless people, and restored splendour to the (true) faith, he proclaimed (pakâsayi) (the treatise called) Kathâvatthu.' And again: 'They all were sectarians[34], opposed to the Theravâda; and in order to annihilate them and to make his own doctrine resplendent, the Thera set forth (desesi) the treatise belonging to the Abhidhamma, which is called Kathâvatthu[35].'

At present, however, we are not concerned with these smaller questions. We treat the canon as a whole, divided into three parts, and containing the books which still exist in MSS., and we want to find out at what time such a collection was made. The following is a short abstract of the Tipiṭaka, chiefly taken from Childers' Pâli Dictionary:

I. Vinaya-piṭaka
1. Vibhaṅga[36].
   Vol. I, beginning with Pârâgika, or sins involving expulsion.
   Vol. II, beginning with Pâkittiya, or sins involving penance.
2. Khandhaka.
   Vol. I, Mahâvagga, the large section.
   Vol. II, Kullavagga, the small section.

3. Parivârapâ*tha*, an appendix and later resumé (25 chapters). See p. xxi, n. 4; p. xxxii, n. 2.

II. Sutta-pi*t*aka

1. Dîgha-nikâya, collection of long suttas (34 suttas)[37].
2. Ma*ggh*ima-nikâya, collection of middle suttas (152 suttas).
3. Sa*m*yutta-nikâya, collection of joined suttas.
4. Aṅguttara-nikâya[38], miscellaneous suttas, in divisions the length of which increases by one.
5. Khuddaka-nikâya[39], the collection of short suttas, consisting of—

   1. Khuddakapâ*tha*, the small texts[40].
   2. Dhammapada, law verses (423)[41].
   3. Udâna, praise (82 suttas).
   4. Itivuttaka, stories referring to sayings of Buddha.
   5. Suttanipâta, 70 suttas[42].
   6. Vimânavatthu, stories of Vimânas, celestial palaces.
   7. Petavatthu, stories of Pretas, departed spirits.
   8. Theragâthâ, stanzas of monks.
   9. Therîgâthâ, stanzas of nuns.
   10. Gâtaka, former births (550 tales)[43].
   11. Niddesa, explanations of certain suttas by Sâriputta.
   12. Pa*t*isambhidâmagga, the road of discrimination, and intuitive insight.
   13. Apadâna[44], legends.
   14. Buddhava*m*sa[44], story of twenty-four preceding Buddhas and of Gotama.
   15. *K*ariyâpi*t*aka[44], basket of conduct, Buddha's meritorious actions[45].

III. Abhidhamma-piṭaka

1. Dhammasaṅgaṇi, numeration of conditions of life[46].
2. Vibhaṅga, disquisitions (18).
3. Kathâvatthupakaraṇa, book of subjects for discussion (1000 suttas).
4. Puggalapaññatti or paññatti, declaration on puggala, or personality.
5. Dhâtukathâ, account of dhâtus or elements.
6. Yamaka, pairs (ten divisions).
7. Paṭṭhânapakaraṇa, book of causes.

Taking this collection as a whole we may lay it down as self-evident that the canon, in its collected form, cannot be older than any of the events related therein.

There are two important facts for determining the age of the Pâli canon, which, as Dr. Oldenberg[47] has been the first to show, should take precedence of all other arguments, viz.

1. That in the Tipiṭka, as we now have it, no mention is made of the so-called Third Council, which took place at Pâṭaliputta, under King Asoka, about 242 B.C.

2. That in the Tipiṭaka, as we now have it, the First Council of Râgagaha (477 B.C.) and the Second Council of Vesâlî (377 B.C.) are both mentioned.

From these two facts it may safely be concluded that the Buddhist canon, as handed down to us, was finally closed after the Second and before, or possibly at, the Third Council. Nay, the fact that the description of the two Councils stands at the very end of the Kullavagga may be taken, as Dr. Oldenberg remarks, as an indication that it was one of the latest literary contributions which obtained canonical authority, while the great bulk of the canon may probably claim a date anterior to the Second Council.

This fact, namely, that the collection of the canon, as a whole, must have preceded the Second Council rests on an argument which does great credit to the ingenuity of Dr. Oldenberg. The Second Council was convoked to consider the ten deviations[48] from the strict discipline of the earliest times. That discipline had been laid down first in the Pâtimokkha rules, then in the commentary now included in the Vibhaṅga, lastly in the Mahâvagga and Kullavagga. The rules as to what was allowed or forbidden to a Bhikkhu were most minute[49], and they were so firmly established that no one could have ventured either to take away or to add anything to them as they stood in the sacred code. In that code itself a distinction is made between the offences which were from the first visited with punishment (pârâgika and pâkittiya) and those misdemeanours and crimes which were put down as punishable at a later time (dukkata and thullakkaya). With these classes the code was considered as closed, and if any doubt arose as to the criminality of certain acts, it could be settled at once by an appeal to the Vinaya-piṭaka. Now it so happens that, with one exception, the ten deviations that had to be considered at the Second Council, are not provided for in the Vinaya-piṭaka; and I quite agree with Dr. Oldenberg's argument that, if they had been mentioned in the Vinayapiṭaka, the Second Council would have been objectless. A mere appeal to chapter and verse in the existing Piṭaka would then have silenced all dissent. On the other side, if it had been possible to add anything to the canon, as it then existed, the ten, or nine, deviations might have been condemned by a few additional paragraphs of the canon, without convoking a new Council.

I think we may be nearly certain, therefore, that we possess the principal portion of the Vinaya-piṭaka as it existed before the Council of Vesâlî.

So far I quite agree with Dr. Oldenberg. But if he proceeds to argue[50] that certain portions of the canon must have been finally settled before even the First Council took place, or was believed to have taken place, I do not think his arguments conclusive. He contends that in the Parinibbâna-sutta, which tells of the last days of Buddha's life, of his death, the cremation of his body, and the distribution of his relics, and of Subhadda's revolt, it would have been impossible to leave out all mention of the First Council, if that Council had then been known. It is true, no doubt, that Subhadda's disloyalty was the chief cause of the First Council, but there was no necessity to mention that Council. On the contrary, it seems to me that the unity of the Parinibbâna-sutta would have been broken if, besides telling of the last days of Buddha, it had also given a full description of the Council. The very title, the Sutta of the Great Decease, would have become inappropriate, if so important a subject as the first Saṅgîti had been mixed up with it. However, how little we may trust to such general arguments, is best shown by the fact that in some very early Chinese renderings of the Hînayâna text of the Mahâparinibbâna-sutta the story is actually carried on to the First Council, two (Nos. 552 and 119) mentioning the rehearsal under Kaśyapa, while the third (No. 118) simply states that the Tipiṭaka was then collected[51].

We must be satisfied therefore, so far as I can see at present, with fixing the date, and the latest date, of a Buddhist canon at the time of the Second Council, 377 B.C. That some works were added later, we know; that many of the treatises included in the canon existed before that Council, can hardly be doubted. The second chapter of the Dhammapada, for instance, is called the Appamâda-vagga, and if the Mahâvaṃsa (p. 25) tells us that at the time when Asoka was converted by Nigrodha, that Buddhist priest explained to him the Appamâdavagga, we can hardly doubt that there existed then a collection (vagga) of verses on Appamâda, such as we now possess in the Dhammapada and in the Saṃyuttanikâya[52].

With regard to the Vinaya, I should even feel inclined to admit, with Dr. Oldenberg, that it must have existed in a more or less settled form before that time. What I doubt is whether such terms as Piṭaka, basket, or Tipiṭaka, the three baskets, i.e. the canon, existed at that early time. They have not been met with, as yet, in any of the canonical books; and if the Dîpavaṃsa (IV, 32) uses the word 'Tipiṭaka,' when describing the First Council, this is due to its transferring new terms to older times. If Dr. Oldenberg speaks of a Dvi-piṭaka[53] as the name of the canon before the third basket, that of the Abhidhamma, was admitted, this seems to me an impossible name, because at the time when the Abhidhamma was not yet recognised as a third part of the canon, the word piṭaka had probably no existence as a technical term[54].

We must always, I think, distinguish between the three portions of the canon, called the basket of the Suttas, the basket of Vinaya, and the basket of Abhidhamma, and the three subjects of Dhamma (sutta), Vinaya, and Abhidhamma, treated in these baskets. The subjects existed and were taught long before the three baskets were definitely arranged. Dhamma had originally a much wider meaning than Sutta-piṭaka. It often means the whole teaching of Buddha; and even when it refers more particularly to the Sutta-piṭaka, we know that the Dhamma there taught deals largely with Vinaya and Abhidhamma doctrines. Even the fact that at the First Council, according to the description given in the Kullavagga, the

Vinaya and Dhamma only were rehearsed, though proving the absence at that time of the Abhidhamma, as a separate Piṭaka, by no means excludes the subject of the Abhidhamma having been taught under the head of Dhamma. In the Mahâkaruṇâpuṇḍarîka-sûtra the doctrine of Buddha is divided into Dharma and Vinaya; the Abhidharma is not mentioned. But the same text knows of all the twelve Dharmapravaḳanâni[55], the 1. Sûtra; 2. Geya; 3. Vyâ-karaṇa; 4. Gâthâ; 5. Udâna; 6. Nidâna; 7. Avadâna; 8. Itivṛittaka; 9. Gâtaka; 10. Vaipulya; 11. Adbhutadharma; 12. Upadeśa; some of these being decidedly metaphysical.

To my mind nothing shows so well the historical character both of the Kullavagga and of Buddhaghosa in the Introduction to his commentary on the Dîgha-nikâya, as that the former, in its account of the First Council, should know of the Vinaya only, as rehearsed by Upâli, and the Dhamma, as rehearsed by Ânanda, while the much later Buddhaghosa, in his account of the First Council[56], divides the Dhamma into two parts, and states that the second part, the Abhidhamma, was rehearsed after the first part, the Dhamma. Between the time of the Kullavagga and the time of Buddhaghosa the Abhidhamma must have assumed its recognised position by the side of Vinaya and Sutta. It must be left to further researches to determine, if possible, the time when the name of piṭaka was first used, and when Tipiṭaka was accepted as the title of the whole canon.

Whenever we see such traces of growth, we feel that we are on historical ground, and in that sense Dr. Oldenberg's researches into the growth of the Vinaya, previous to the Second Council, deserve the highest credit. He shows, in opposition to other schol-ars, that the earliest elements of Vinaya must be looked for in the short Pâtimokkha rules, which were afterwards supplemented by explanations, by glosses and commentaries, and in that form answered for some time every practical purpose. Then followed a new generation who, not being satisfied, as it would seem, with these brief rules and comments, wished to know the occasion on which these rules had been originally promulgated. What we now call the Vibhanga, i.e. the first and second divisions of the Vinaya-pitaka, is a collection of the stories, illustrating the origin of each rule, of the rules themselves (the Pâtimokkha), and of the glosses and comments on these rules.

The third and fourth books, the Mahâvagga and Kullavagga, are looked upon as possibly of a slightly later date. They treat, in a similar manner as the Vibhanga, on the rules not included in that collection, and give a general picture of the outward life of the monks. While the Vibhanga deals chiefly with the original so-called pârâgika, sanghâdisesa, and pâkittîya offences, the Khandhaka, i.e. the Mahâvagga and Kullavagga, treats of the so-called dukkata and thullakkaya crimes. The arrangement is the same, story, rule, and comment succeeding each other in regular sequence.

If we follow the guidance of the Vinaya-pitaka, we should be able to distinguish the following steps in the growth of Buddhism before the Second Council of Vesâlî:

1. Teaching of Buddha and his disciples (543/477 A.D. Buddha's death).
2. Collection of Pâtimokkha rules (first code).
3. Comment and glosses on these rules.
4. Stories in illustration of these rules (vibhanga).
5. Mahâvagga and Kullavagga (Khandhaka).
6. Council of Vesâlî for the repression of ten abuses (443/377 A.D.)

7. Description of First and Second Councils in *Kullavagga*.
    The *Kullavagga* ascribes the settlement of the canon to
    the First Council, and does not even claim a revision
    of that canon for the Second Council. The Dîpava*m*sa
    claims a revision of the canon by the 700 Arhats for the
    Second Council.

Chronology

In order to bring the Council of Vesâlî in connection with the
chronology of the world, we must follow the Buddhist historians for another century. One hundred and eighteen years after
the Council of Vesâlî they place the anointment of King Asoka,
during whose reign a Third Council, under the presidency of
Tissa Moggaliputta, took place at Pâ*t*aliputta, the new capital adopted by that king, instead of Râgagaha and Vesâlî. This Council
is chiefly known to us through the writings of the southern Buddhists (Dîpava*m*sa, Mahâva*m*sa, and Buddhaghosa), who belong to
the school of Moggaliputta (Theravâda or Vibha*gg*avâda), which
ruled supreme at Pâ*t*aliputta, while Upagupta, the chief authority of the northern Buddhists, is altogether ignored in the Pâli
chronicles.

Now it is well known that Asoka was the grandson of *K*andagutta, and *K*andagutta the contemporary of Alexander the
Great. Here we see land, and I may refer to my History of Sanskrit Literature, published in 1859, for the process by which the
storm-tossed ship of Indian chronology has been landed in the
harbour of real historical chronology. We are told by the monks
of the Mahâvihâra in Ceylon that Asoka was crowned, according
to their computation, 146 + 18 years before the accession of Du*t*-

*tha*gâmani, 161 B.C., i.e. 325 B.C.; that between his coronation and his father's death four years had elapsed (329 B.C.); that his father Bindusâra had reigned twenty-eight years[57] (357–329 B.C.), and Bindusâra's father, Kandagutta, twenty-four years (381–357). As we know that Kandagutta, whom the Ceylonese place 381–357 B.C., was king of India after Alexander's conquest, it follows that Ceylonese chronology is wrong by more than half a century. For reasons stated in my History of Sanskrit Literature, I fix the exact fault in Ceylonese chronology as sixty-six years, assigning to Kandagutta the dates 315–291, instead of 381–357. This gives us 291–263 for Bindusâra, 259 for Asoka's abhisheka; 259 + 118 = 377 for the Council of Vesâlî, and 377 + 100 = 477 for Buddha's death, instead of 543 B.C.[58]

These dates are, of course, approximate only, and they depend on one or two points on which people may differ. But, with that reservation, I see no ground whatever for modifying the chronological system which I put forward more than twenty years ago. Professor Westergaard and Professor Kern, who have since suggested different dates for the death of Buddha, do not really differ from me in principle, but only in their choice of one or the other alternative, which I readily admit as possible, but not as more certain than my own. Professor Westergaard[59], for instance, fixes Buddha's death at 368 (370), instead of 477. This seems a wide difference, but it is so in appearance only.

Following Justinus, who says that Sandrokyptos[60] had conquered the empire of India at the time when Seleucus laid the foundations of his own greatness, I had accepted 315[61], half-way between the murder of Porus and the taking of Babylon by Seleucus, as the probable beginning of Kandragupta's reign. Westergaard prefers 320 as a more likely date for Kandragupta, and therefore places the death of the last Nanda and the beginning of Asoka's royal pretensions 268. Here there is a difference between him and me of five years, which depends chiefly on the view we take as to the time when Seleucus really laid what Justinus calls the foundation of his future greatness. Secondly, Westergaard actually adopts the idea, at which I only hinted as possible, that the southern Buddhists made two Asokas out of one, and two Councils out of one. Trusting in the tradition that 118 years elapsed between Buddha's death and the Council under Asoka (at Pâtaliputra), and that the Council took place in the king's tenth year (as was the case with the imaginary Kâlâsoka's Council), he gets $268 - 10 = 258$ as the date of the Council, and 368 or 370 as the date of Buddha's death[62].

The two points on which Westergaard differs from me, seem to me questions which should be kept before our mind in dealing with early Buddhist history, but which, for the present at least, admit of no definite solution.

The same remark seems to me to apply to the calculations of another eminent Sanskrit scholar, Professor Kern[63]. He lays great stress on the general untrustworthiness of Indian chronology, and I am the last to differ from him on that point. He then places the beginning of Kandragupta's reign in 322 B.C. Allowing twenty-four years to him and twenty-eight to his son Bindusâra, he places the beginning of Asoka's reign in 270. Asoka's inscriptions would fall about 258. As Asoka reigned thirty-six or thirty-seven years, his death would fall in 234 or 233 B.C. Like Westergaard, Professor Kern too eliminates Kâlâsoka, as a kind of chronological Asoka, and the Council of Vaisâlî, and therefore places Buddha's death, according to the northern tradition, 100 or 110 years before Dharmâsoka, i.e. 270 + 100 or + 110 = 370 or 380[64]; while, according to the southern tradition, that 118 years elapsed between Asoka's accession and Buddha's death, the Ceylonese monks would seem originally to have retained 270 + 118[65] = 388 B.C. as Buddha's Nirvâna, a date which, as Professor Kern holds, happens to coincide with the date assigned to the death of Mahâvîra, the founder of the Gaina religion.

Here we see again that the moot point is the beginning of Kandragupta's reign in accordance with the information supplied by Greek historians. Professor Kern places it in 322, Westergaard in 320, I myself in 315. That difference once granted, Dr. Kern's reasoning is the same as my own. According to the traditions which we follow, Buddha's death took place 100, 110, 118, or 228 years before Asoka. Hence Professor Westergaard arrives at 368 or 370 B.C. Professor Kern at 370 (380) or 388 B.C., I myself at 477 B.C. Every one of these dates is liable to certain objections, and if I prefer my own date, 477 B.C., it is simply because it seems to me liable to neither more nor less reservations than those of Professor Westergaard and Professor Kern, and because, so long as we always remember the grounds of our differences, namely, the beginning of Kandragupta's reign, and the additional century, every one of these dates furnishes a good hypothesis to work on, until we can arrive at greater certainty in the ancient chronology of India.

To my mind all dates beyond Kandragupta are as yet purely tentative, resting far more on a chronological theory than on actual tradition; and though I do not doubt the historical character of the Council of Vaisâlî, I look upon the date assigned to it, on the authority of the Dîpavaṃsa and Mahâvaṃsa, as, for the present, hypothetical only.

B.C.

557. Buddha born.

552. Bimbisâra born.

537–485. Bimbisâra, founder of Râgagṛiha, 5 years younger than Buddha, was 15 when crowned, 30 or 31 when he met Buddha in 522.

485–453. Agâtasatru (4 × 8 years).

477. Buddha's death (485 − 8 = 477).

477. COUNCIL AT RÂGAGṚIHA, under Kâśyapa, Ânanda, and Upâli.

453–437. Udâyibhadra, founder of Pâṭaliputra (2 × 8 years).

437–429. {Anuruddhaka (8 years).
Muṇda (at Pâṭaliputra).

429–405. Nâgadâsaka (3 × 8 years).

405–387. Siśunâga (at Vaiśâlî).

387–359. Kâlâśoka.

377. COUNCIL AT VAIŚÂLÎ, under Yaśas and Revata, a disciple of Ânanda (259 + 118 = 377).

359–337. Ten sons of Kâlâśoka (22 years).

337–315. Nine Nandas (22 years); the last, Dhanananda, killed by Kâṇakya.

315–291. Kandragupta (477 − 162 = 315; 3 × 8 years)[66]; Megasthenes, ambass. of Seleucus.

291–263. Bindusâra (Amitrochates).

263–259. Asoka, sub-king at Uggayinî, as pretender—his brothers killed; Daimachus, ambass. of Antiochus, son of Seleucus; Dionysius, ambass. of Ptolemy II.

259. Asoka anointed at Pâṭaliputra, H. Ths. I, 160 (477 − 218 = 259).

256. Asoka converted by Nigrodha (D.V. vi, 18).

256–253. Building of Vihâras, Sthûpas, &c.

255. Conversion of Tishya (M.V. p. 34).

253. Ordination of Mahendra (born 477 − 204 = 273).

251. Tishya and Sumitra die (D.V. VII, 32).

242. COUNCIL AT PÂṬALIPUTRA (259 − 17 = 242; 477 − 236 = 241), under Tishya Maudgalîputra (477 − 236 = 241; D.V. VII, 37).

241. Mahendra to Ceylon.

222. Asoka died (259 − 37 = 222).

193. Mahendra died (D.V. XVII, 93).

161. Duṭṭhagâmani.

88–76. Vattagâmani, canon reduced to writing.

A.D.

400. Dîpavaṃsa.

420. Buddhaghosha, Pâli commentaries, 30 years later Devardhigaṇina, Jacobi, p. 16.

459–477. Mahâvaṃsa.

Though the preceding table, embodying in the main the results at which I arrived in my History of Ancient Sanskrit Literature, still represents what I hold to be true or most probable with respect to Indian chronology, previous to the beginning of our era, yet I suppose I may be expected to say here a few words on the two latest attempts to fix the date of Buddha's death; the one by Mr. Rhys Davids in the Numismata Orientalia, Part VI, 1877, the other by Dr. Bühler in the Indian Antiquary, 1877 and 1878[67]. Mr. Rhys Davids, to whom we owe so much for the elucidation of the history of Buddha's religion, accepts Westergaard's date for the beginning of Kandragupta's reign, 320 B.C., instead of 322 (Kern), 315 (myself); and as he assigns (p. 41) to Bindusâra 25 years instead of 28 (Mahâvamsa, p. 21), he arrives at 268 as the year of Asoka's coronation[68]. He admits that the argument derived from the mention of the five foreign kings in one of Asoka's inscriptions, dated the twelfth year of his reign, is too precarious to enable us to fix the date of Asoka's reign more definitely, and though, in a general way, that inscription confirms the date assigned by nearly all scholars to Asoka in the middle of the third century B.C., yet there is nothing in it that Asoka might not have written in 247 quite as well as in 258–261. What chiefly distinguishes Mr. Rhys Davids' chronology from that of his predecessors is the shortness of the period between Asoka's coronation and Buddha's death. On the strength of an examination of the list of kings and the list of the so-called patriarchs, he reduces the traditional 218 years to 140 or 150, and thus arrives at 412 B.C. as the probable beginning of the Buddhist era.

In this, however, I cannot follow him, but prefer to follow Dr. Bühler. As soon as I saw Dr. Bühler's first essay on the Three New Edicts of Asoka, I naturally felt delighted at the unexpected confirmation which he furnished of the date which I had assigned to Buddha's death, 477 B.C. And though I am quite aware of the danger of unexpected confirmations of one's own views, yet, after carefully weighing the objections raised by Mr. Rhys Davids and Professor Pischel against Dr. Bühler's arguments, I cannot think that they have shaken Dr. Bühler's position. I fully admit the difficulties in the phraseology of these inscriptions: but I ask, Who could have written these inscriptions, if not Asoka? And how, if written by Asoka, can the date which they contain mean anything but 256 years after Buddha's Nirvâna? These points, however, have been argued in so masterly a manner by Dr. Bühler in his 'Second Notice,' that I should be afraid of weakening his case by adding anything of my own, and must refer my readers to his 'Second Notice.' Allowing that latitude which, owing to the doubtful readings of MSS., and the constant neglect of odd months, we must allow in the interpretation of Buddhist chronology, Asoka is the only king we know of who could have spoken of a thirty-fourth year since the beginning of his reign and since his conversion to Buddhism. And if he calls that year, say the very last of his reign (222 B.C.), 256. after the departure of the Master, we have a right to say that as early as Asoka's time, Buddha was believed to have died about 477 B.C. Whether the inscriptions have been accurately copied and rightly read is, however, a more serious question, and the doubts raised by Dr. Oldenberg (Mahâvagga, p. xxxviii) make a new collation of the originals absolutely indispensable, before we can definitely accept Dr. Bühler's interpretation.

I cannot share Dr. Bühler's opinion[69] as to the entire worthlessness of the Gaina chronology in confirming the date of Buddha's death. If the Svetâmbara Gainas place the death of Mahâvîra 470 before Vikramâditya, i.e. 56 B.C. + 470 = 526 B.C., and the Digambaras 605, i.e. 78 A.D. deducted from 605 = 527 B.C., this so far confirms Dr. Bühler's and Dr. Jacobi's brilliant discovery that Mahâvîra was the same as Nigantha Nâtaputta, who died at Pâvâ during Buddha's lifetime[70]. Most likely 527 is too early a date, while another tradition fixing Mahâvîra's death 155 years before Kandragupta[71], 470 B.C., is too late. Yet they both show that the distance between Asoka (259–222 B.C.), the grandson of Kandragupta (315–291 B.C.), and the contemporaries of Buddha was by the Gainas also believed to be one of two rather than one century.

When I saw that the date of Buddha's death, 477 B.C., which in my History of Ancient Sanskrit Literature (1859) I had myself tried to support by such arguments as were then accessible, had received so powerful a support by the discovery of the inscriptions of Sahasrâm, Rûpnâth, and Bairât, due to General Cunningham, who had himself always been an advocate of the date 477 B.C., and through their careful decipherment by Dr. Bühler, I lost no time in testing that date once more by the Dîpavaṃsa, that Ceylonese chronicle having lately become accessible through Dr. Oldenberg's edition and translation[72]. And here I am able to say that, before having read Dr. Bühler's Second Notice, I arrived, though by a somewhat different way, at nearly the same conclusions as those so well worked out by Dr. Bühler in his restoration of the Episcopal Succession (therâvali) of the Buddhists, and therefore feel convinced that, making all such allowances as the case requires, we know now as much of early Buddhist chronology as could be known at the time of Asoka's Council, 242 B.C.

Taking the date of Buddha's death 477 B.C. for granted, I found that Upâli, who rehearsed the Vinaya at the First Council, 477 B.C., had been in orders sixty years in the twenty-fourth year of Agâtasatru, i.e. 461 B.C., which was the sixteenth year A.B. He must therefore[73] have been born in 541 B.C., and he died 447 B.C., i.e. thirty years A.B., at the age of 94. This is said to have been the sixth year of Udâyi, and so it is, 453 − 6 = 447 B.C.

In the year 461 B.C. Dâsaka received orders from Upâli, who was then 80 years of age; and when Dâsaka had been in orders forty-five years (Dîpava*m*sa IV, 41), he ordained Saunaka. This would give us 461 − 45 = 416 B.C., while the tenth year of Nâgadâsa, 429 − 10, would give us 419 A.D. Later on the Dîpava*m*sa (V, 78) allows an interval of forty years between the ordinations of Dâsaka and Saunaka, which would bring the date of Saunaka's ordination to 421 B.C., instead of 419 or 416 B.C. Here there is a fault which must be noted. Dâsaka died 461 − 64 = 397 A.D., which is called the eighth year of Sisunâga, and so it is, 405 − 8 = 397 A.D.

When Saunaka had been in orders forty years, i.e. 416 − 40 = 376, Kâlâsoka is said to have reigned a little over ten years, i.e. 387 − 11 = 376 A.D., and in that year Saunaka ordained Siggava. He died 416 − 66 − 350 A.D., which is called the sixth year of the Ten, while in reality it is the ninth, 359 − 6 = 353 A.D. If, however, we take 419 as the year of Saunaka's ordination, his death would fall 419 − 66 = 353 B.C.

Siggava, when he had been in orders sixty-four years, ordained Tishya Maudgalîputra. This date 376 − 64 = 312 B.C. is called more than two years after Kandragupta's accession, and so it very nearly is, 315 − 2 = 313.

Siggava died when he had been in orders seventy-six years, i.e. 376 − 76 = 300 A.D. This year is called the fourteenth year of Kandragupta, which it very nearly is, 315 − 14 = 301.

When Tishya had been in orders sixty[74] years, he ordained Mahendra, 312 − 60 = 252 B.C. This is called six years after Asoka's coronation, 259 − 6 = 253, and so it very nearly is. He died 312 − 80 = 232 B.C., which is called the twenty-sixth year of Asoka, and so it very nearly is.

Buddhist Patriarchs

	Birth.	Ordination.	Ordination of successor.	Death.	Age.	Patri- archate.
Upâli	(Generally 20 years before ordination)	527 (60)	461	447	94	30
Dâsaka	"	461 45⎫ 42⎬ 40⎭	416⎫ 419⎬ 421⎭	397	84	50
Saunaka	"	416⎫ 419⎬ 421⎭ (40)	376⎫ 379⎬ 381⎭	350 353	86	44 (47)
Siggava	"	376½ (64)	312½	300½	96	50 (52)
Tishya	"	312½ (60)	253	233	100	68
Mahendra	273	253	"	193	80	40
						282 (284)

If we test the dates of this table by the length of time assigned to each patriarchate, we find that Upâli ruled thirty years, from Buddha's death, 477 to 447; Dâsaka fifty years. To Saunaka forty-four years are assigned, instead of forty-seven, owing to a fault pointed out before; and to Siggava fifty-two years, or fifty-five[75] instead of fifty. Tishya's patriarchate is said to have lasted sixty-eight years, which agrees with previous statements.

Lastly, the years of the death of the six patriarchs, as fixed according to the reigns of the kings of Magadha, agree extremely well.

Upâli died in the sixth year of Udâyi, i.e. 453 − 6 = 447 B.C.

Dâsaka died in the eighth year of Sisunâga, i.e. 405 − 8 = 397 B.C.

Saunaka died in the sixth year of the Ten, i.e. 359 − 6 = 353 B.C., showing again the difference of three years.

Siggava died in the fourteenth year of Kandragupta, i.e. 315 − 14 = 301 B.C.

Tishya died in the twenty-sixth or twenty-seventh year of Asoka, i.e. 259 − 27 = 233 B.C.

This general and more than general agreement between dates taken from the history of the kings and the history of the patriarchs leaves on my mind a decided impression of a tradition which, though not strictly historical, in our sense of the word, represents at all events the result of such enquiries as could be made into the past ages of Buddhism at the time of Asoka. There are difficulties in that tradition which would certainly have been avoided, if the whole chronology had been simply made up: but there is no doubt a certain method perceptible throughout, which warns us that we must not mistake a smooth chronology for solid history.

The Title of Dhammapada

The title of Dhammapada has been interpreted in various ways. It is an ambiguous word, and has been accepted as such by the Buddhists themselves. Dhamma has many meanings. Under one aspect it means religion, particularly the religion taught by Buddha, the law which every Buddhist should accept and observe. Under another aspect dhamma is virtue, or the realisation of the law.

Pada also has many meanings. In the Abhidhâna-padîpikâ it is explained by place, protection, Nirvâna, cause, word, thing, portion, foot, footstep.

Hence dhammapada may mean 'footstep of religion,' and thus the title was first rendered by Gogerly, only that he used the plural instead of the singular, and called it 'The Footsteps of Religion,' while Spence Hardy still more freely called it 'The Paths of Religion.' It may be quite true, as pointed out by Childers, that pada by itself never means path. But it means footstep, and the footstep towards a thing is much the same as what we call the path to a thing. Thus we read, verse 21, 'appamâdo amatapadam,' earnestness is the step, i.e. the path that leads to immortality. Again, 'pamâdo makkuno padam' can hardly mean anything but that thoughtlessness is the path of death, is the path that leads to death. The commentator, too, rightly explains it here by amatasya adhigamupâya, the means of obtaining immortality, i.e. Nirvâna, or simply by upâyo, and even by maggo, the way. If we compare verses 92 and 93 of our text, and verses 254 and 255, we see that pada is used synonymously with gati, going. In the same manner dhammapada would mean the footstep or the footpath of virtue, i.e. the path that leads to virtue, and supply a very appropriate title for a collection of moral precepts. In verses 44 and 45 'path of virtue' seems to be the most appropriate meaning for dhammapada[76], and it is hardly possible to assign any other meaning to it in the following verse (Kundasutta, v. 6):

> *Yo dhammapade sudesite*
> *Magge gîvati saññato satimâ,*
> *Anavagga-padâni sevamâno*
> *Tatîyam bhikkhum âhu maggagîvim,*

'He who lives restrained and attentive in the way that has been well pointed out, in the path of the law, cultivating blameless words, such a Bhikkhu they call a Maggagîvi (living in the way).'

I therefore think that 'Path of Virtue,' or 'Footstep of the Law,' was the idea most prominent in the mind of those who originally framed the title of this collection of verses. It seems to me that Buddhaghosa also took the same view, for the verse which D'Alwis[77] quotes from the introduction of Buddhaghosa's commentary,—

Sampatta-saddhammapado satthâ dhammapada*m* subha*m*
Desesi,

and which he translates, 'The Teacher who had reached the very depths (lit. bottom) of Saddhamma, preached this holy Dhammapada,'—lends itself far better to another translation, viz. 'The Teacher who had gained a firm footing in the Good Law, showed (preached) the holy Path of the Law.'

Gogerly, again, who may generally be taken as a faithful representative of the tradition of the Buddhists still preserved in Ceylon, translates the title by the 'Footsteps of Religion,' so that there can be little doubt that the priests of that island accept Dhammapada in the sense of 'Vestiges of Religion,' or, from a different point of view, 'The Path of Virtue.'

M. L. Feer[78] takes a slightly different view, and assigning to pada the meaning of foot or base, he translates Dhammapada by Loi fondamentale, or Base de la Religion.

But it cannot be denied that the title of Dhammapada was very soon understood in a different sense also, namely, as 'Sentences of Religion.' Pada means certainly a foot of a verse, a verse, or a line, and dhammapadam actually occurs in the sense of a 'religious sentence.' Thus we read in verse 102, 'Though a man recite a hundred Gâthâs made up of senseless words, one dhammapadam, i.e. one single word or line of the law, is better, which if a man hears, he becomes quiet.' But here we see at once the difficulty of translating the title of 'dhammapadam' by 'religious sentences.' Dhammapadam means one law verse, or wise saw, not many. Professor Fausböll, who in his excellent edition of the Dhammapada translated that title by 'a collection of verses on religion,' appeals to such passages as verses 44 and 102 in support of his interpretation. But in verse 42 dhammapadam sudesitam, even if it does not mean the path of the law, could never mean 'versus legis bene enarratos,' but only versum legis bene enarratum, as Dr. Fausböll himself renders ekam dhammapadam, in verse 102, by unus legis versus. Buddhaghosa, too, when he speaks of many law verses uses the plural, for instance[79], 'Be it known that the Gâthâ consists of the Dhammapadâni, Theragâthâ, Therîgâthâ, and those unmixed (detached) Gâthâ not comprehended in any of the above-named Suttânta.'

The only way in which Dhammapada could be defended in the sense of 'Collection of Verses of the Law,' would be if we took it for an aggregate compound. But such aggregate compounds, in Sanskrit at least, are possible with numerals only; for instance, tribhuvanam, the three worlds; katuryugam, the four ages[80]. It might therefore be possible in Pâli, too, to form such compounds as dasapadam, a collection of ten padas, a work consisting of ten padas, a decamerone, but it would in no wise follow that we could in that language attempt such a compound as Dhammapadam, in order to express a collection of law verses[81]. Mr. Beal[82] informs us that the Chinese seem to have taken Dhammapada in the sense of 'stanzas of law,' 'law texts,' or 'scripture texts.'

It should be remembered, also, that the idea of representing life, and particularly the life of the faithful, as a path of duty or virtue leading to deliverance, (in Sanskrit dharmapatha,) is very familiar to Buddhists. The four great truths of their religion[83] consist in the recognition of the following principles: 1. that there is suffering; 2. that there is a cause of that suffering; 3. that such cause can be removed; 4. that there is a way of deliverance, viz. the doctrine of Buddha. This way is the ashtânga-mârga, the eightfold way[84], taught by Buddha, and leading to Nirvâna[85]. The faithful advances on that road, padât padam, step by step, and it is therefore called patipadâ, lit. the step by step.

If we make allowance for these ambiguities, inherent in the name of Dhammapada, we may well understand how the Buddhists themselves play with the word pada (see v. 45). Thus we read in Mr. Beal's translation of a Chinese version of the Prâtimoksha[86]:

'Let all those who desire such birth,
Who now are living in the world,
Guard and preserve these Precepts, as feet.'

Translation

In translating the verses of the Dhammapada, I have followed the edition of the Pâli text, published in 1855 by Dr. Fausböll, and I have derived great advantage from his Latin translation, his notes, and his copious extracts from Buddhaghosa's commentary. I have also consulted translations, either of the whole of the Dhammapada, or of portions of it, by Burnouf, Gogerly[87], Upham, Weber, and others. Though it will be seen that in many places my translation differs from those of my predecessors, I can only claim for myself the name of a very humble gleaner in this field of Pâli literature. The greatest credit is due to Dr. Fausböll; and though later critics have been able to point out some mistakes, both in his text and in his translation, the value of their labours is not to be compared with that of the work accomplished single-handed by that eminent Danish scholar.

In revising my translation, first published in 1870[88], for the Sacred Books of the East, I have been able to avail myself of 'Notes on Dhammapada,' published by Childers in the Journal of the Royal Asiatic Society (May, 1871), and of valuable hints as to the meaning of certain words and verses scattered about in the Pâli Dictionary of that much regretted scholar, 1875. I have carefully weighed the remarks of Mr. James D'Alwis in his 'Buddhist Nirvâna, a review of Max Müller's Dhammapada' (Colombo, 1871), and accepted some of his suggestions. Some very successful renderings of a number of verses by Mr. Rhys Davids in his 'Buddhism,' and a French translation, too, of the Dhammapada, published by Fernand Hû[89], have been consulted with advantage.

It was hoped for a time that much assistance for a more accurate understanding of this work might be derived from a Chinese translation of the Dhammapada[90], of which Mr. S. Beal published an English translation in 1878. But this hope has not been entirely fulfilled. It was, no doubt, a discovery of great interest, when Mr. Beal announced that the text of the Dhammapada was not restricted to the southern Buddhists, but that similar collections existed in the north, and had been translated into Chinese. It was equally important when Schiefner proved the existence of the same work in the sacred canon of the Tibetans. But as yet neither a Chinese nor a Tibetan translation of the Pâli Dhammapada has been rendered accessible to us by translations of these translations into English or German, and what we have received instead, cannot make up for what we had hoped for.

The state of the case is this. There are, as Mr. Beal informs us, four principal copies of what may be called Dhammapada in Chinese, the first dating from the Wu dynasty, about the beginning of the third century A.D. This translation, called Fa-kheu-king, is the work of a Shaman Wei-*k*i-lan and others. Its title means 'the Sûtra of Law verses,' kheu being explained by gâthâ, a verse, a word which we shall meet with again in the Tibetan title, Gâthâsangraha. In the preface the Chinese translator states that the Shamans in after ages copied from the canonical scriptures various gâthâs, some of four lines and some of six, and attached to each set of verses a title, according to the subject therein explained. This work of extracting and collecting is ascribed to Tsun-*ke*-Fa-kicou, i.e. Ârya-Dharmatrâta, the author of the Samyuktâbhi-dharma-sâstra and other works, and the uncle of Vasumitra. If this Vasumitra was the patriarch who took a prominent part in the Council under Kanishka, Dharmatrâta's collection would belong to the first century B.C.; but this is, as yet, very doubtful.

In the preface to the Fa-kheu-king we are told that the original, which consisted of 500 verses, was brought from India by Wai-*k*i-lan in 223 A.D., and that it was translated into Chinese with the help of another Indian called Tsiangsin. After the translation was finished, thirteen sections were added, making up the whole to 752 verses, 14,580 words, and 39 chapters[91].

If the Chinese translation is compared with the Pâli text, it appears that the two agree from the 9th to the 35th chapter (with the exception of the 33rd), so far as their subjects are concerned, though the Chinese has in these chapters 79 verses more than the Pâli. But the Chinese translation has eight additional chapters in the beginning (viz. On Intemperance, Inciting to Wisdom, The Srâvaka, Simple Faith, Observance of Duty, Reflection, Loving-kindness, Conversation), and four at the end (viz. Nirvâna, Birth and Death, Profit of Religion, and Good Fortune), and one between the 24th and 25th chapter of the Pâli text (viz. Advantageous Service), all of which are absent in our Pâli texts. This, the most ancient Chinese translation of Dharmatrâta's work, has not been rendered into English by Mr. Beal, but he assures us that it is a faithful reproduction of the original. The book which he has chosen for translation is the Fa-kheu-pi-ü, i.e. parables connected with the Dhammapada, and translated into Chinese by two Shamans of the western Tsin dynasty (A.D. 265–313). These parables are meant to illustrate the teaching of the verses, like the parables of Buddhaghosa, but they are not the same parables, nor do they illustrate all the verses.

A third Chinese version is called Kuh-yan-king, i.e. the Sûtra of the Dawn (avadâna?), consisting of seven volumes. Its author was Dharmatrâta, its translator Ku-fo-nien (Buddhasmriti), about 410 A.D. The MS. of the work is said to have been brought from India by a Shaman Sangha-bhadanga of Kipin (Cabul), about 345 A.D. It is a much more extensive work in 33 chapters, the last being, as in the Pâli text, on the Brâhmana.

A fourth translation dates from the Sung dynasty (800 or 900 A.D.), and in it, too, the authorship of the text is ascribed to Ârya-Dharmatrâta.

A Tibetan translation of a Dhammapada was discovered by Schiefner in the 28th volume of the Sûtras, in the collection called

Udânavarga. It contains 33 chapters, and more than 1000 verses, of which about one-fourth only can be traced in the Pâli text. The same collection is found also in the Tangur, vol. 71 of the Sûtras, foll. 1–53, followed by a commentary, the Udânavarga-vivarana by the Âkârya Pragñâvarman. Unfortunately Schiefner's intention of publishing a translation of it (Mélanges Asiatiques, tom. viii, p. 560) has been frustrated by his death. All that he gives us in his last paper is the Tibetan text with translation of another shorter collection, the Gâthâsangraha by Vasubandhu, equally published in the 72nd volume of the Sûtras in the Tangur, and accompanied by a commentary.

Spelling of Buddhist Terms

I had on a former occasion[92] pleaded so strongly in favour of retaining, as much as possible, the original Sanskrit forms of Pâli Buddhist terms, that I feel bound to confess openly that I hold this opinion no longer, or, at all events, that I see it is hopeless to expect that Pâli scholars will accept my proposal. My arguments were these: 'Most of the technical terms employed by Buddhist writers come from Sanskrit; and in the eyes of the philologist the various forms which they have assumed in Pâli, in Burmese, in Tibetan, in Chinese, in Mongolian, are only so many corruptions of the same original form. Everything, therefore, would seem to be in favour of retaining the Sanskrit forms throughout, and of writing, for instance, Nirvâna instead of the Pâli Nibbâna, the Burmese Niban or Nepbhân, the Siamese Niruphan, the Chinese Nipan. The only hope, in fact, that writers on Buddhism will ever arrive at a uniform and generally intelligible phraseology seems to lie in their agreeing to use throughout the Sanskrit terms in their original form, instead of the various local disguises and disfigurements which they present in Ceylon, Burmah, Siam, Tibet, China, and Mongolia.'

I fully admitted that many Buddhist words have assumed such a strongly marked local or national character in the different countries and in the different languages in which the religion of Buddha has found a new home, that to translate them back into Sanskrit might seem as affected, nay, prove in certain cases as misleading, as if, in speaking of priests and kings, we were to speak of presbyters and cynings. The rule by which I meant mainly to be guided was to use the Sanskrit forms as much as possible; in fact, everywhere except where it seemed affected to do so. I therefore wrote Buddhaghosha instead of the Pâli Buddhaghosa, because the name of that famous theologian, 'the Voice of Buddha,' seemed to lose its significance if turned into Buddhaghosa. But I was well aware what may be said on the other side. The name of Buddhaghosa, 'Voice of Buddha,' was given him after he had been converted from Brahmanism to Buddhism, and it was given to him by people to whom the Pâli word ghosa conveyed the same meaning as ghosha does to us. On the other hand, I retained the Pâli Dhammapada instead of Dharmapada, simply because, as the title of a Pâli book, it has become so familiar that to speak of it as Dharmapada seemed like speaking of another work. We are accustomed to speak of Samanas instead of Sramanas, for even in the days of Alexander's conquest, the Sanskrit word Sramana had assumed the prakritized or vulgar form which we find in Pâli, and which alone could have been rendered by the later Greek writers (first by Alexander Polyhistor, 80–60 B.C.) by σαμαναῖοι[93]. As a Buddhist term, the Pâli form Samana has so entirely supplanted that of Sramana that, even in the Dhammapada

(v. 388), we find an etymology of Samana as derived from sam, 'to be quiet,' and not from *sram*, 'to toil.' But if we speak of Samanas, we ought also to speak of Bâhma*n*as instead of Brâhma*n*as, for this word had been replaced by bâhma*n*a at so early a time, that in the Dhammapada it is derived from a root vah, 'to remove, to separate, to cleanse[94].'

I still believe that it would be best if writers on Buddhist literature and religion were to adopt Sanskrit throughout as the lingua franca. For an accurate understanding of the original meaning of most of the technical terms of Buddhism a knowledge of their Sanskrit form is indispensable; and nothing is lost, while much would be gained, if, even in the treating of southern Buddhism, we were to speak of the town of *Srâvastî* instead of Sâvatthi in Pâli, Sevet in Sinhalese; of Tripi*t*aka, 'the three baskets,' instead of Tip-i*t*aka in Pâli, Tunpitaka in Sinhalese; of Arthakathâ, 'commentary,' instead of A*tth*akathâ in Pâli, Atuwâva in Sinhalese; and therefore also of Dharmapada, 'the path of virtue,' instead of Dhammapada.

But inclinations are stronger than arguments. Pâli scholars prefer their Pâli terms, and I cannot blame them for it. Mr. D'Alwis (Buddhist Nirvâ*n*a, p. 68) says: 'It will be seen how very difficult it is to follow the rule rigidly. We are, therefore, inclined to believe that in translating Pâli works, at least, much inconvenience may not be felt by the retention of the forms of the language in which the Buddhist doctrines were originally delivered.' For the sake of uniformity, therefore, I have given up my former plan. I use the Pâli forms when I quote from Pâli, but I still prefer the Sanskrit forms, not only when I quote from Sanskrit Buddhist books, but also when I have to speak of Buddhism in general. I speak of Nirvâ*n*a, dharma, and bhikshu, rather than of Nibbâna, dhamma, and bhikkhu, when discussing the meaning of these words without special reference to southern Buddhism; but when treating of the literature and religion of the Theravâda school I must so far yield to the arguments of Pâli scholars as to admit that it is but fair to use their language when speaking of their opinions.

1

The Twin-Verses

1. All that we are is the result of what we have thought: it is founded on our thoughts, it is made up of our thoughts. If a man speaks or acts with an evil thought, pain follows him, as the wheel follows the foot of the ox that draws the carriage.

2. All that we are is the result of what we have thought: it is founded on our thoughts, it is made up of our thoughts. If a man speaks or acts with a pure thought, happiness follows him, like a shadow that never leaves him.

3. 'He abused me, he beat me, he defeated me, he robbed me,'—in those who harbour such thoughts hatred will never cease.

4. 'He abused me, he beat me, he defeated me, he robbed me,'—in those who do not harbour such thoughts hatred will cease.

5. For hatred does not cease by hatred at any time: hatred ceases by love, this is an old rule.

6. The world does not know that we must all come to an end here;—but those who know it, their quarrels cease at once.

7. He who lives looking for pleasures only, his senses uncontrolled, immoderate in his food, idle, and weak, Mâra (the tempter) will certainly overthrow him, as the wind throws down a weak tree.

8. He who lives without looking for pleasures, his senses well controlled, moderate in his food, faithful and strong, him Mâra will certainly not overthrow, any more than the wind throws down a rocky mountain.

9. He who wishes to put on the yellow dress without having cleansed himself from sin, who disregards also temperance and truth, is unworthy of the yellow dress.

10. But he who has cleansed himself from sin, is well grounded in all virtues, and endowed also with temperance and truth, he is indeed worthy of the yellow dress.

11. They who imagine truth in untruth, and see untruth in truth, never arrive at truth, but follow vain desires.

12. They who know truth in truth, and untruth in untruth, arrive at truth, and follow true desires.

13. As rain breaks through an ill-thatched house, passion will break through an unreflecting mind.

14. As rain does not break through a well-thatched house, passion will not break through a well-reflecting mind.

15. The evil-doer mourns in this world, and he mourns in the next; he mourns in both. He mourns and suffers when he sees the evil (result) of his own work.

16. The virtuous man delights in this world, and he delights in the next; he delights in both. He delights and rejoices, when he sees the purity of his own work.

17. The evil-doer suffers in this world, and he suffers in the next; he suffers in both. He suffers when he thinks of the evil he has done; he suffers more when going on the evil path.

18. The virtuous man is happy in this world, and he is happy in the next; he is happy in both. He is happy when he thinks of the good he has done; he is still more happy when going on the good path.

19. The thoughtless man, even if he can recite a large portion (of the law), but is not a doer of it, has no share in the priesthood, but is like a cowherd counting the cows of others.

20. The follower of the law, even if he can recite only a small portion (of the law), but, having forsaken passion and hatred and foolishness, possesses true knowledge and serenity of mind, he,

caring for nothing in this world or that to come, has indeed a share in the priesthood.

---

1. Dharma, though clear in its meaning, is difficult to translate. It has different meanings in different systems of philosophy, and its peculiar application in the phraseology of Buddhism has been fully elucidated by Burnouf, Introduction à l'Histoire du Buddhisme, p. 41 seq. He writes: 'Je traduis ordinairement ce terme par condition, d'autres fois par lois, mais aucune de ces traductions n'est parfaitement complète; il faut entendre par dharma ce qui fait qu'une chose est ce qu'elle est, ce qui constitue sa nature propre, comme l'a bien montré Lassen, à l'occasion de la célèbre formule, "Ye dharmâ hetuprabhavâ,"' Etymologically the Latin for-ma expresses the same general idea which was expressed by dhar-ma. See also Burnouf, Lotus de la bonne Loi, p. 524. Fausböll translates: 'Naturae a mente principium ducunt,' which shows that he rightly understood dharma in the Buddhist sense. Gogerly (see Spence Hardy, Eastern Monachism, p. 28) translates: 'Mind precedes action,' which, if not wrong, is at all events wrongly expressed; while Professor Weber's rendering, 'Die Pflichten aus dem Herz folgern,' is not admissible. D'Alwis (Buddhist Nirwana, p. 70 seq.), following the commentary, proposes to give a more technical interpretation of this verse, viz. 'Mind is the leader of all its faculties. Mind is the chief (of all its faculties). The very mind is made up of those (faculties). If one speaks or acts with a polluted mind, then affliction follows him as the wheel follows the feet of the bearer (the bullock).' To me this technical acceptation seems not applicable here, where we have to deal with the simplest moral precepts, and not with psychological niceties of Buddhist philosophy. It should be stated, however, that Childers, who first (s.v. dhamma) approved of my translation, seems afterwards to have changed his opinion. On p. 120 of his excellent Pâli Dictionary he said: 'Three of the five khandhas, viz. vedanâ, saññâ, and saṅkhâra, are collectively termed dhammâ (plur.), "mental faculties," and in the first verse of Dhammapada the commentator takes the word dhammâ to mean those three faculties. But this interpretation appears forced and unnatural, and I look upon Dr. Max Müller's translation, "All that we are is the result of what we have thought," as the best possible rendering of the spirit of the phrase mano pubbaṅgamâ dhammâ.' But on p. 577 the same scholar writes: 'Of the four mental khandhas the superiority of viññâna is strongly asserted in the first verse of Dhammapada, "The mental faculties (vedanâ, saññâ, and saṅkhâra) are dominated by Mind, they are governed by Mind, they are made up of Mind."That this is the true meaning of the passage I am now convinced; see D'Alwis, Nirwana, pp. 70–75.' I do not deny that this may have been the traditional interpretation, at all events since the days of Buddhaghosa,

but the very legend quoted by Buddhaghosa in illustration of this verse shows that its simpler and purely moral interpretation was likewise supported by tradition, and I therefore adhere to my original translation. See also v. 109.

2. See Beal, Dhammapada, p. 169.

3. On akko*kkh*i, see Ka*kk*âyana VI, 4, 17. D'Alwis, Pâli Grammar, p. 38 note. 'When akko*kkh*i means "he abused," it is derived from kru*s*, not from krudh.' See Senart, Ka*kk*âyana, l.c.

On upanayhati=upanandhati, see J. P.T. S. 1887, p. 126; it would mean literally he who ties up such thoughts, that is he who holds fast to them.

5. Sanantana, translated by Childers by 'perpetual, ancient, primeval,' cf. Sk. sana, sanâ, sanât, sanâtana. Buddhaghosa explains it by porâ*n*aka.

6. Pare is explained by 'fools,' but it has that meaning by implication only. It is οἱ πολλοί, cf.Vinaya, ed. Oldenberg, vol. i, p. 5, l. 4.Yamâmase, a 1 pers. plur. imp. Âtm., but really a Le*t* in Pâli. See Fausböll, Five Gâtakas, p. 38. Weber translates, 'Wir sollen uns bezähmen hier,' which may be right, but differs from Buddhaghosa.

7. Mâra must be taken in the Buddhist sense of 'tempter,' or 'evil spirit.' See Burnouf, Introduction, p. 76: 'Mâra est le démon de l'amour, du péché et de la mort; c'est le tentateur et l'ennemi de Buddha.' As to the definite meaning of vîrya, see Burnouf, Lotus, p. 548.

In the Buddhistical Sanskrit, kusîda, 'idle,' is the exact counterpart of the Pâli kusîta; see Burnouf, Lotus, p. 548. On the change of Sanskrit d into Pâli t, see Kuhn, Beiträge zur Pali Grammatik, p. 40; Weber, Ind. Studien, XIII, p. 135.

9. The dark yellow dress, the Kâsâva or Kâshâya, is the distinctive garment of the Buddhist priests. See Vish*n*u-sûtra LXIII, 36. The play on the words anikkasâvo kâsâvam, or in Sanskrit anishkashâya*h* kâshâyam, cannot be rendered in English. Kashâya means 'impurity,' nish-kashâya, 'free from impurity,' anish-kashâya, 'not free from impurity,' while kâshâya is the name of the yellowish Buddhist garment. The pun is evidently a favourite one, for, as Fausböll shows, it occurs also in the Mahâbhârata, XII, 568:

Anishkashâye kâshâyam îhârtham iti viddhi tam,
Dharmadhvagânâ*m* mu*nd*ânâm vrittyartham iti me mati*h*.

'Know that this yellow-coloured garment on a man who is not free from impurity, serves only for the purpose of cupidity; my opinion is, that it is meant to supply the means of living to those shavelings, who carry their virtue or the dharma like a flag.'

(I read v*r*ittyartham, according to the Bombay edition, instead of k*r*itârtham, the reading of the Calcutta edition.)

On the exact colour of the dress, see Bishop Bigandet, The Life or Legend of Gaudama, the Budha of the Burmese, Rangoon, 1866, p. 504. Cf. Gâtaka, vol. ii, p. 198.

10. With regard to sîla, 'virtue,' see Burnouf, Lotus, p. 547.

11, 12. Sâra, which I have translated by 'truth,' has many meanings in Sanskrit. It means the sap of a thing, then essence or reality; in a metaphysical sense, the highest reality; in a moral sense, truth. It is impossible in a translation to do more than indicate the meaning of such words, and in order to understand them fully, we must know not only their definition, but their history. See Beal, Dhammapada, p. 64.

13. See Beal, Dhammapada, p. 65.

15. Kili*tt*ha is klish*t*a, a participle of kli*s*. It means literally, what is spoilt. The abstract noun kle*s*a, 'evil or sin,' is constantly employed in Buddhist works; see Burnouf, Lotus, p. 443.

16. Like klish*t*a in the preceding verse, vi*s*uddhi in the present has a technical meaning. One of Buddhaghosa's most famous works is called Visuddhi-magga. See Burnouf, Lotus, p. 844; Beal, Dhammapada, p. 67.

17, 18. 'The evil path and the good path' are technical expressions for the descending and ascending scale of worlds through which all beings have to travel upward or downward, according to their deeds; see Bigandet, Life of Gaudama, p. 5, note 4, and p. 449; Burnouf, Introduction, p. 599; Lotus, p. 865, l. 7; l. 11. Fausböll translates 'heaven and hell,' which comes to the same; cf. vv. 126, 306.

19. In taking sahitam in the sense of sa*m*hitam or sa*m*hitâ, I follow the commentator who says, Tepi*t*akassa Buddhava*k*anass' eta*m* nâma*m*, but I cannot find another passage where the Tipi*t*aka, or any portion of it, is called Sahita. Sa*m*hita in vv. 100–102 has a different meaning. The fact that some followers of Buddha were allowed to learn short portions only of the sacred writings by heart, and to repeat them, while others had to learn a larger collection, is shown by the story of *K*akkhupâla, p. 3, of Mahâkâla, p. 26, &c. See Childers, s.v. sahita.

20. Sâma*ññ*a, which I have rendered by 'priesthood,' expresses all that belongs to, or constitutes a real Sama*n*a or *S*rama*n*a, this being the Buddhist name corresponding to the Brâhma*n*a, or priest, of the orthodox Hindus. Buddha himself is frequently called the Good Sama*n*a. Fausböll takes the abstract word sâma*ññ*a as corresponding to the Sanskrit sâmânya, 'community,' but Weber has well shown that it ought to be taken as representing *s*râma*n*ya. He might have quoted the Sâma*ññ*a-phala-sutta, of which Burnouf has given such interesting details in his Lotus, p. 449 seq. Fausböll also, in his notes on v. 332, rightly explains sâma*ññ*atâ by *s*râma*n*yatâ. See Childers, s.v. sâma*ññ*a.

Anupâdiyâno, which I have translated by 'caring for nothing,' has a technical meaning. It is the negative of the fourth Nidâna, the so-called Upâdâna, which Köppen has well explained by Anhänglichkeit, 'clinging to the world, loving the world.' Köppen, Die Religion des Buddha, p. 610. Cf. Suttanipâta, v. 470.

On huram, see J. P. T. S., 1884, p. 103 seq.

2

On Earnestness[1]

21. Earnestness is the path of immortality (Nirvâna), thoughtlessness the path of death. Those who are in earnest do not die, those
who are thoughtless are as if dead already.

22. Having understood this clearly, those who are advanced in
earnestness delight in earnestness, and rejoice in the knowledge
of the Ariyas (the elect).

23. These wise people, meditative, steady, always possessed of
strong powers, attain to Nirvâna, the highest happiness.

24. If an earnest person has roused himself, if he is not forgetful,
if his deeds are pure, if he acts with consideration, if he restrains
himself, and lives according to law,—then his glory will increase.

25. By rousing himself, by earnestness, by restraint and control,

the wise man may make for himself an island which no flood can overwhelm.

26. Fools follow after vanity, men of evil wisdom. The wise man keeps earnestness as his best jewel.

27. Follow not after vanity, nor after the enjoyment of love and lust! He who is earnest and meditative, obtains ample joy.

28. When the learned man drives away vanity by earnestness, he, the wise, climbing the terraced heights of wisdom, looks down upon the fools, free from sorrow he looks upon the sorrowing crowd, as one that stands on a mountain looks down upon them that stand upon the plain.

29. Earnest among the thoughtless, awake among the sleepers, the wise man advances like a racer, leaving behind the hack.

30. By earnestness did Maghavan (Indra) rise to the lordship of the gods. People praise earnestness; thoughtlessness is always blamed.

31. A Bhikshu (mendicant) who delights in earnestness, who looks with fear on thoughtlessness, moves about like fire, burning all his fetters, small or large.

32. A Bhikshu (mendicant) who delights in reflection, who looks with fear on thoughtlessness, cannot fall away (from his perfect state)—he is close upon Nirvâna.

21. Apramâda, which Fausböll translates by 'vigilantia,' Gogerly by 'religion,' Childers by 'diligence,' expresses literally the absence of that giddiness or thoughtlessness which characterizes the state of mind of worldly people. It is the first entering into oneself, and hence all virtues are said to have their root in apramâda. (Ye keki kusalâ dhammâ sabbe te appamâdamûlakâ.) I have translated it by 'earnestness,' sometimes by 'reflection.' 'Immortality,' amrita, is explained by Buddhaghosa as Nirvâna. Amrita is used, no doubt, as a synonym of Nirvâna, but this very fact shows how many different conceptions entered from the very first into the Nirvâna of the Buddhists. See Childers, s.v. nibbâna, p. 269.

This verse, as recited to Asoka, occurs in the Dîpavazmsa VI, 53, and in the Mahâvamsa, p. 25. See also Sanatsugâtîya, translated by Telang, Sacred Books of the East, vol. viii, p. 138.

22. The Ariyas, the noble or elect, are those who have entered on the path that leads to Nirvâna; see Köppen, p. 396. Their knowledge and general status is fully described; see Köppen, p. 436.

23. Childers, s.v. nibbâna, thinks that nibbâna here and in many other places means Arhatship.

25. Childers explains this island again as the state of an Arhat (arahatta-phalam).

28. Cf. Childers, Dictionary, Preface, p. xiv. See Vinaya, ed. Oldenberg, vol. i, p. 5, s. f.

31. Instead of saham, which Dr. Fausböll translates by 'vincens,' Dr. Weber by 'conquering,' I think we ought to read dahan, 'burning,' which was evidently the reading adopted by Buddhaghosa. Mr. R. C. Childers, whom I requested to see whether the MS. at the India Office gives saham or daham, writes that the reading daham is as clear as possible in that MS. Prof. Fausböll also now writes that my conjecture is confirmed by his own MSS. also. Mr. Neumann, however, retains saham. The fetters are meant for the senses. See verse 370.

32. See Childers, Notes, p. 5.

3

Thought

33. As a fletcher makes straight his arrow, a wise man makes straight his trembling and unsteady thought, which is difficult to guard, difficult to hold back,

34. As a fish taken from his watery home and thrown on the dry ground, our thought trembles all over in order to escape the dominion of Mâra (the tempter).

35. It is good to tame the mind, which is difficult to hold in and flighty, rushing wherever it listeth; a tamed mind brings happiness.

36. Let the wise man guard his thoughts, for they are difficult to perceive, very artful, and they rush wherever they list: thoughts well guarded bring happiness.

37. Those who bridle their mind which travels far, moves about alone, is without a body, and hides in the chamber (of the heart), will be free from the bonds of Mâra (the tempter).

38. If a man's faith is unsteady, if he does not know the true law, if his peace of mind is troubled, his knowledge will never be perfect.

39. If a man's thoughts are not dissipated, if his mind is not perplexed, if he has ceased to think of good or evil, then there is no fear for him while he is watchful.

40. Knowing that this body is (fragile) like a jar, and making his thought firm like a fortress, one should attack Mâra (the tempter) with the weapon of knowledge, one should watch him when conquered, and should never rest.

41. Before long, alas! this body will lie on the earth, despised, without understanding, like a useless log.

42. Whatever a hater may do to a hater, or an enemy to an enemy, a wrongly-directed mind will do him greater mischief.

43. Not a mother, not a father will do so much, nor any other relatives; a well-directed mind will do us greater service.

---

33. *Kitta*, here translated by thought, may be rendered also by mind or heart. It is, however, incorporeal, dwells in the heart, and is opposed to the body, see Ab. 152, 338. Cf. Gâtaka, vol. i, p. 400.

34. On Mâra, see verses 7 and 8.

35–39. Cf. Gâtaka, vol. i, pp. 312, 400.

39. Fausböll traces anavassuta, 'dissipated,' back to the Sanskrit root *syai*, 'to become rigid;' but the participle of that root would be *sîta*, not *syuta*. Professor Weber suggests that anavassuta stands for the Sanskrit anavasruta, which he translates unbefleckt, 'unspotted.' If avasruta were the right word, it might be taken in the sense of 'not fallen off, not fallen away,' but it could not mean 'unspotted;' cf. dhairya*m* no *x* susruvat, 'our firmness ran away.' I have little doubt, however, that avassuta represents the Sanskrit avasruta, and is derived from the root *sru*, here used in its technical sense, peculiar to the Buddhist literature, and so well explained by Burnouf in his Appendix XIV (Lotus, p. 820). He shows that, according to Hema*k*andra and the *G*ina-alankâra, âsravakshaya, Pâli âsavasa*m*khaya is counted as the sixth abhig*ñ*â, wherever six of these intellectual powers are mentioned, instead of five. The Chinese translate the term in their own Chinese fashion by 'stillationis finis,' but Burnouf claims for it the definite sense of destruction of faults or vices. He quotes from the Lalita-vistara (Adhyâya XXII, ed. Râjendra Lal Mittra, p. 448) the words uttered by Buddha when he arrived at his complete Buddhahood:—

*Sushkâ âsravâ na puna*h *sravanti,*
'The vices are dried up, they will not flow again;'

and he shows that the Pâli Dictionary, the Abhidhânappadîpikâ, explains âsava simply by kâma, 'love, pleasure of the senses.' In the Mahâparinibbâna-sutta, three classes of âsava are distinguished, the kâmâsavâ, the bhavâsavâ, and the avi*gg*âsavâ. See also Burnouf, Lotus, p. 665; Childers, s.v. âsavo.

That *sru* means 'to run,' and is in fact a merely dialectic variety of sru, has been proved by Burnouf, while Boehtlingk thinks the substitution of *s* for s is a mistake. Â*s*rava therefore, or âsrava, meant originally 'the running out towards objects of the senses' (cf. sanga, âlaya, &c.), and had nothing to do with âsrâva, 'a running, a sore,' Atharva-veda I, 2, 4. This conception of the original purport of â + *s*ru or ava-*s*ru is confirmed by a statement of Colebrooke's, who, when treating of the *G*ainas, writes (Miscellaneous Essays, I, 382): 'Âsrava is that which directs the embodied spirit (âsravayati purusham) towards external objects. It is the occupation and employment (v*ri*tti or prav*ri*tti) of the senses or organs on sensible objects. Through the means of the senses it affects the embodied spirit with the sentiment of taction, colour, smell, and taste. Or it is the association or connection of body with right and wrong deeds. It comprises all the karmas, for they (âsravayanti) pervade, influence, and attend the doer, following him or attaching to him. It is a misdirection (mithyâ-prav*ri*tti) of the organs, for it is vain, a cause of disappointment, rendering the organs of sense and sensible objects subservient to fruition. Sa*m*vara is that which stops (samvrinoti) the course of the foregoing, or closes up the door or passage to it, and consists in self-command or restraint of organs internal and external, embracing all means of self-control and subjection of the senses, calming and subduing them.'

For a full account of the âsravas, see Lalita-vistara, ed. Calc. pp. 445 and 552, where Kshînâsrava is given as a name of Buddha. Âsrâva occurs in Âpastamba's Dharma-sûtras II, 5, 9, where the commentator explains it by objects of the senses, by which the soul is made to run out. It is better, however, to take âsrâva here, too, as the act of running out, the affections, appetites, passions.

40. Anivesana has no doubt a technical meaning, and may signify, one who has left his house, his family and friends, to become a monk. A monk shall not return to his home, but travel about; he shall be anivesana, 'homeless,' anâgâra, 'houseless.' But I doubt whether this can be the meaning of anivesana here, as the sentence, let him be an anchorite, would come in too abruptly. I translate it therefore in a more general sense, let him not return or turn away from the battle, let him watch Mâra, even after he is vanquished, let him keep up a constant fight against the adversary, without being attached to anything or anybody.

43. See Beal, Dhammapada, p. 73.

4

Flowers[1]

44. Who shall overcome this earth, and the world of Yama (the lord of the departed), and the world of the gods? Who shall find out the plainly shown path of virtue, as a clever man finds the (right) flower?

45. The disciple will overcome the earth, and the world of Yama, and the world of the gods. The disciple will find out the plainly shown path of virtue, as a clever man finds the (right) flower.

46. He who knows that this body is like froth, and has learnt that it is as unsubstantial as a mirage, will break the flower-pointed arrow of Mâra, and never see the king of death.

47. Death carries off a man who is gathering flowers, and whose mind is distracted, as a flood carries off a sleeping village.

48. Death subdues a man who is gathering flowers, and whose mind is distracted, before he is satiated in his pleasures.

49. As the bee collects nectar and departs without injuring the flower, or its colour or scent, so let a sage dwell in his village.

50. Not the perversities of others, not their sins of commission or omission, but his own misdeeds and negligences should a sage take notice of.

51. Like a beautiful flower, full of colour, but without scent, are the fine but fruitless words of him who does not act accordingly.

52. But, like a beautiful flower, full of colour and full of scent, are the fine and fruitful words of him who acts accordingly.

53. As many kinds of wreaths can be made from a heap of flowers, so many good things may be achieved by a mortal when once he is born.

54. The scent of flowers does not travel against the wind, nor (that of) sandal-wood, or (of) Tagara and Mallikâ flowers; but the odour of good people travels even against the wind; a good man pervades every place.

55. Sandal-wood or Tagara, a lotus-flower, or a Vassikî, among these sorts of perfumes, the perfume of virtue is unsurpassed.

56. Mean is the scent that comes from Tagara and sandal-wood;—

the perfume of those who possess virtue rises up to the gods as the highest.

57. Of the people who possess these virtues, who live without thoughtlessness, and who are emancipated through true knowledge, Mâra, the tempter, never finds the way.

58, 59. As on a heap of rubbish cast upon the highway the lily will grow full of sweet perfume and delight, thus among those who are mere rubbish the disciple of the truly enlightened Buddha shines forth by his knowledge above the blinded worldling.

44, 45. If I differ from the translation of Fausböll and Weber, it is because the commentary takes the two verbs, vigessati and pakessati, to mean in the end the same thing, i.e. sakkhi-karissati, 'he will perceive.' I have not ventured to take vigessate for viganissali, though it should be remembered that the overcoming of the earth and of the worlds below and above, as here alluded to, is meant to be achieved by means of knowledge. Pakessati, 'he will gather' (cf. vi-ki, Indische Sprüche, 4560), means also, like 'to gather' in English, 'he will perceive or understand,' and the dhammapada, or 'path of virtue,' is distinctly explained by Buddhaghosa as consisting of the thirty-seven states or stations which lead to Bodhi. (See Burnouf, Lotus, p. 430; Hardy, Manual, p. 497.) Dhammapada might, no doubt, mean also 'a law-verse,' and sudesita, 'well taught,' and this double meaning may be intentional here as elsewhere. Buddha himself is called Mârga-darsaka and Mârga-desika (cf. Lal.Vist. p. 551). There is a curious similarity between these verses and verses 6540–41, and 9939 of the Sântiparva:

Pushpânîva vikinvantam anyatragatamanasam,
Anavâpteshu kâmeshu mrityur abhyeti mânavam.

'Death approaches man like one who is gathering flowers, and whose mind is turned elsewhere, before his desires have been fulfilled.'

Suptam vyâghram mahaugho vâ mrityur âdâya gakkhati,
Sankinvânakam evainam kâmânâm avitriptikam.

'As a stream (carries off) a sleeping tiger, death carries off this man who is gathering flowers, and who is not satiated in his pleasures.'

This last verse, particularly, seems to me clearly a translation from Pâli, and the kam of saṅkinvânakam looks as if put in metri causâ. See also verse 12063.

46. The flower-arrows of Mâra, the tempter, are borrowed from Kâma, the Hindu god of love. For a similar expression see Lalita-vistara, ed. Calc. p. 40, l. 20, mâyâmarîkisadrisâ vidyutphenopamâs kapalâh. It is on account of this parallel passage that I prefer to translate marîki by 'mirage,' and not by 'sunbeam,' as Fausböll, or by 'solar atom,' as Weber proposes. The expression, 'he will never see the king of death,' is supposed to mean Arhatship by Childers, s.v. nibbâna, p. 270.

47. See Thiessen, Die Legende von Kisâgotamî, p. 9.

48. Antaka, 'death,' is given as an explanation of Mâra in the Amarakosha and Abhidhânappadîpika (cf. Fausböll, p. 210).

49. See Beal, Catena, p. 159, where vv. 49 and 50 are ascribed to Wessabhu, i.e. Visvabhû. See also Der Weise und der Thor, p. 134.

See Fausböll, Nogle Bemerkninger. Buddhaghosa renders ahethayam by avinâsento; and Kern, Verhandelingen der Koninkligke Akademie, Amsterdam, 1888, p. 19.

51. St. Matthew xxiii. 3, 'For they say, and do not.'

54. Tagara, a plant from which a scented powder is made. Mallaka or mallikâ, according to Benfey, is an oil vessel. Hence tagaramallikâ was supposed to mean a bottle holding aromatic powder, or oil made of the Tagara. Mallikâ, however, is given by Dr. Eitel (Handbook of Chinese Buddhism) as the name of a flower now called Casturi (musk) on account of its rich odour, and Dr. Morris informs me that he has found mallikâ in Pâli as a name of jasmine. See also Childers, s.v.; Notes, p. 6; and Beal, Dhammapada, p. 76.

58, 59. Cf. Beal, Dhammapada, p. 76.

5

The Fool

60. Long is the night to him who is awake; long is a mile to him who is tired; long is life to the foolish who do not know the true law.

61. If a traveller does not meet with one who is his better, or his equal, let him firmly keep to his solitary journey; there is no companionship with a fool.

62. 'These sons belong to me, and this wealth belongs to me,' with such thoughts a fool is tormented. He himself does not belong to himself; how much less sons and wealth?

63. The fool who knows his foolishness, is wise at least so far. But a fool who thinks himself wise, he is called a fool indeed.

64. If a fool be associated with a wise man even all his life, he will perceive the truth as little as a spoon perceives the taste of soup.

65. If an intelligent man be associated for one minute only with a wise man, he will soon perceive the truth, as the tongue perceives the taste of soup.

66. Fools of poor understanding have themselves for their greatest enemies, for they do evil deeds which bear bitter fruits.

67. That deed is not well done of which a man must repent, and the reward of which he receives crying and with a tearful face.

68. No, that deed is well done of which a man does not repent, and the reward of which he receives gladly and cheerfully.

69. As long as the evil deed done does not bear fruit, the fool thinks it is like honey; but when it ripens, then the fool suffers grief.

70. Let a fool month after month eat his food (like an ascetic) with the tip of a blade of Kusa grass, yet is he not worth the sixteenth particle of those who have well weighed the law.

71. An evil deed, like newly-drawn milk, does not turn (suddenly); smouldering, like fire covered by ashes, it follows the fool.

72. And when the evil deed, after it has become known, turns to sorrow for the fool, then it destroys his bright lot, nay, it cleaves his head.

73. Let the fool wish for a false reputation, for precedence among the Bhikshus, for lordship in the convents, for worship among other people!

74. 'May both the layman and he who has left the world think that this is done by me; may they be subject to me in everything which is to be done or is not to be done,' thus is the mind of the fool, and his desire and pride increase.

75. 'One is the road that leads to wealth, another the road that leads to Nirvâna;' if the Bhikshu, the disciple of Buddha, has learnt this, he will not yearn for honour, he will strive after separation from the world.

---

60. 'Life,' samsâra, is the constant revolution of birth and death which goes on for ever until the knowledge of the true law or the true doctrine of Buddha enables a man to free himself from samsâra, and to enter into Nirvâna. See Buddhaghosha's Parables, Parable XIX, p. 134.

61. Cf. Suttanipâta, v. 46.

63. Cf. Beal, Dhammapada, p. 77.

64. The same verses occur in the Mahâbh. Sauptikap. v. 178; see also Sabhâp. v. 1945.

65. Cf. Beal, Dhammapada, p. 78.

67. See Beal, l.c. p. 78.

69. Taken from the Samyutta-nikâya, where, however, we read thânanhi instead of madhuvâ; see Feer, Comptes Rendus, 1871, p. 64.

70. The commentator clearly takes sankhâta in the sense of sankhyâta, 'reckoned,' for he explains it by ñâtadhammâ, tulitadhammâ. The eating with the tip of Kusa grass has reference to the fastings performed by the Brâhmans, but disapproved of, except as a moderate discipline, by the followers of Buddha. This verse seems to interrupt the continuity of the other verses which treat of the reward of evil deeds, or of the slow but sure ripening of every sinful act. See Childers, s.v. sankhâto.

71. I am not at all certain of the simile, unless mukkati, as applied to milk, can be used in the sense of changing or turning sour. In Manu IV, 172, where a similar sentence occurs, the commentators are equally doubtful: Nâdharmas karito loke sadyah phalati gaur iva, 'for an evil act committed in the world does not bear fruit at once, like a cow;' or 'like the earth (in due season);' or 'like milk.' See Childers, Notes, p. 6.

72. I take ñattam for gñapitam, the causative of gñâtam, for which in Sanskrit, too, we have the form without i, gñaptam. This gñaptam, 'made known, revealed,'

stands in opposition to the *kh*anna, 'covered, hid,' of the preceding verse. Sukka*m*sa, which Fausböll explains by *s*uklâ*m*sa, has probably a more technical and special meaning. Childers traces *ñ*attam to the Vedic *gñ*âtram, 'knowledge.' Fausböll refers to Gâtaka, vol. i, p. 445, v. 118.

75. Viveka, which in Sanskrit means chiefly understanding, has several meanings with the Buddhists, and among them the more technical meaning of separation, whether separation from the world and retirement to the solitude of the forest (kâya-viveka), or separation from idle thoughts (*k*itta-viveka), or the highest separation and freedom (Nirvâ*n*a). As true knowledge cannot be said to be a road to wealth, I have taken a*ññ*a, not for âg*ñ*â, but for anyâ.

6

The Wise Man (Pandita)

76. If you see a man who shows you what is to be avoided, who administers reproofs, and is intelligent, follow that wise man as you would one who tells of hidden treasures; it will be better, not worse, for him who follows him.

77. Let him admonish, let him teach, let him forbid what is improper!—he will be beloved of the good, by the bad he will be hated.

78. Do not have evil-doers for friends, do not have low people for friends: have virtuous people for friends, have for friends the best of men.

79. He who drinks in the law lives happily with a serene mind: the sage rejoices always in the law, as preached by the elect (Ariyas).

80. Well-makers lead the water (wherever they like); fletchers bend the arrow; carpenters bend a log of wood; wise people fashion themselves.

81. As a solid rock is not shaken by the wind, wise people falter not amidst blame and praise.

82. Wise people, after they have listened to the laws, become serene, like a deep, smooth, and still lake.

83. Good men indeed walk (warily) under all circumstances; good men speak not out of a desire for sensual gratification; whether touched by happiness or sorrow wise people never appear elated or depressed.

84. If, whether for his own sake, or for the sake of others, a man wishes neither for a son, nor for wealth, nor for lordship, and if he does not wish for his own success by unfair means, then he is good, wise, and virtuous.

85. Few are there among men who arrive at the other shore (become Arhats); the other people here run up and down the shore.

86. But those who, when the law has been well preached to them, follow the law, will pass over the dominion of death, however difficult to cross.

87, 88. A wise man should leave the dark state (of ordinary life), and follow the bright state (of the Bhikshu). After going from his home to a homeless state, he should in his retirement look for enjoyment where enjoyment seemed difficult. Leaving all pleasures behind, and calling nothing his own, the wise man should purge himself from all the troubles of the mind.

89. Those whose mind is well grounded in the (seven) elements of knowledge, who without clinging to anything, rejoice in freedom from attachment, whose appetites have been conquered, and who are full of light, they are free (even) in this world.

---

78. It is hardly possible to take mitte kalyâne in the technical sense of kalyâna-mitra, 'ein geistlicher Rath,' a spiritual guide. Burnouf (Introd. p. 284) shows that in the technical sense kalyânamitra was widely spread in the Buddhist world.

79. Ariya, 'elect, venerable,' is explained by the commentator as referring to Buddha and other teachers.

80. See verses 33 and 145, the latter being a mere repetition of our verse. The nettikâs, to judge from the commentary and from the general purport of the verse, are not simply water-carriers, but builders of canals and aqueducts, who force the water to go over the fields where it would not go by itself. The Chinese translator says, 'the pilot manages his ship.' See Beal, l.c. p. 79.

83. The first line is very doubtful. Mr. Childers writes, 'I think it will be necessary to take sabbattha in the sense of "everywhere," or "under all circumstances;" pañkakhandâdibhedesu, sabbadhammesu, says Buddhaghosa. I do not think we need assume that B. means the word vigahanti to be a synonym of vaganti. I would rather take the whole sentence together as a gloss upon the word vaganti:—vagantîti arahattañânena apakaddhantâ khandarâgam vigahanti; vaganti means that, ridding themselves of lust by the wisdom which Arhatship confers, they cast it away.' The line means 'the righteous walk on (unmoved) in all the conditions of life.' Nindâ, pasamsâ, sukha, dukkha are four of the eight lokadhammas, or earthly conditions; the remaining lokadhammas are lâbha, alâbha, yasa, ayasa. I have adopted the translation of W. Morris, see Journal of P. T. S., 1891–93, p. 41.

In v. 245, passatâ, 'by a man who sees,' means 'by a man who sees clearly or truly.' In the same manner vrag may mean, not simply 'to walk,' but 'to walk properly,' or may be used synonymously with pravrag.

84. That the last line forms the apodosis is shown by the demonstrative pronoun sa.

85. 'The other shore' is meant for Nirvâna, 'this shore' for common life. On reaching Nirvâna, the dominion of death is overcome. The commentator supplies târitvâ, 'having crossed,' in order to explain the accusative ma*kk*udheyyam, but possibly pâram essanti should here be taken as one word, in the sense of overcoming.

87, 88. Dark and bright are meant for bad and good; cf. Suttanipâta, v. 526, and Dhp. v. 167. Leaving one's home is the same as becoming a mendicant, without a home or family, an anâgâra, or anchorite. A man in that state of viveka, or retirement (see v. 75, note), sees, that where before there seemed to be no pleasure there real pleasure is to be found, or vice versâ. A similar idea is expressed in verse 99. See Burnouf, Lotus, p. 474, where he speaks of 'Le plaisir de la satisfaction, né de la distinction.' On pariyodapeyya, see Childers, s.v.

The five troubles or evils of the mind are passion, anger, ignorance, arrogance, pride; see Burnouf, Lotus, pp. 360, 443. As to pariyodapeyya, see verse 183, and Lotus, pp. 523, 528; as to aki*ñk*ano, see Mahâbh. XII, 6568, 1240.

89. The elements of knowledge are the seven Sambodhyaṅgas, on which see Burnouf, Lotus, p. 796. D'Alwis explains them as the thirty-seven Bodhipakkhiya-dhammâ. Khînâsavâ, which I have translated by 'they whose frailties have been conquered,' may also be taken in a more metaphysical sense, as explained in the note to v. 39. The same applies to the other terms occurring in this verse, such as âdâna, anupâdâya, &c. Dr. Fausböll seems inclined to take âsava in this passage, and in the other passages where it occurs, as the Pâli representative of âsraya. But âsraya, in Buddhist phraseology, means rather the five organs of sense with manas, 'the soul,' and these are kept distinct from the âsavas, 'the inclinations, the appetites, passions, or vices.' The commentary on the Abhidharma, when speaking of the Yogâkâras, says, 'En réunissant ensemble les réceptacles (âsraya), les choses reçues (âsrita) et les supports (âlambana), qui sont chacun composés de six termes, on a dix-huit termes qu'on appelle "Dhâtus" ou contenants. La collection des six réceptacles, ce sont les organes de la vue, de l'ouïe, de l'odorat, du goût, du toucher, et le "manas" (ou l'organe du cœur), qui est le dernier. La collection des six choses reçues, c'est la connaissance produite par la vue et par les autres sens jusqu'au "manas" inclusivement. La collection des six supports, ce sont la forme et les autres attributs sensibles jusqu'au "Dharma" (la loi ou l'être) inclusivement.' See Burnouf, Introduction, p. 449.

Parinibbuta is again a technical term, the Sanskrit parinivrita meaning 'freed from all worldly fetters,' like vimukta. See Burnouf, Introduction, p. 590. See Childers, s.v. nibbâna, p. 270, and Notes on Dhammapada, p. 3; and D'Alwis, Buddhist Nirvâna, p. 75.

7

The Venerable (Arhat)

90. There is no suffering for him who has finished his journey, and abandoned grief, who has freed himself on all sides, and thrown off all fetters.

91. They exert themselves with their thoughts well-collected, they do not tarry in their abode; like swans who have left their lake, they leave their house and home.

92. Men who have no riches, who live on recognised food, who have perceived void and unconditioned freedom (Nirvâna), their path is difficult to understand, like that of birds in the air.

93. He whose appetites are stilled, who is not absorbed in enjoyment, who has perceived void and unconditioned freedom (Nirvâna), his path is difficult to understand, like that of birds in the air.

94. The gods even envy him whose senses, like horses well broken in by the driver, have been subdued, who is free from pride, and free from appetites;

95. Such a one who does his duty is tolerant like the earth, or like a threshold; he is like a lake without mud; no new births are in store for him.

96. His thought is quiet, quiet are his word and deed, when he has obtained freedom by true knowledge, when he has thus become a quiet man.

97. The man who is free from credulity, but knows the uncreated, who has cut all ties, removed all temptations, renounced all desires, he is the greatest of men.

98. In a hamlet or in a forest, on sea or on dry land, wherever venerable persons (Arahanta) dwell, that place is delightful

99. Forests are delightful; where the world finds no delight, there the passionless will find delight, for they look not for pleasures.

---

91. Satîmanto, Sanskrit smritimantah, 'possessed of memory,' but here used in the technical sense of sati, the first of the Bodhyangas. See Burnouf, Introduction, p. 797. Clough translates it by 'intense thought,' and this is the original meaning of smar, even in Sanskrit. See Lectures on the Science of Language, vol. ii, p. 332.

Uyyuñganti, which Buddhaghosa explains by 'they exert themselves,' may possibly signify 'they depart,' i.e. they leave their family, and embrace an ascetic life. See note to verse 235. See also Rhys Davids, Mahâparinibbâna-sutta, Sacred Books of the East, vol. xi, p. 22.

92. Suññato and animitto are adjectives belonging to vimokho, one of the many names of Nirvâna, or, according to Childers, s.v. nibbâna, p. 270, Arhatship;

see Burnouf, Introduction, pp. 442, 462, on sûnya. The Sanskrit expression sûnyatânimittâpraṇihitam occurs in L'enfant egaré, 5 a, l. 4. Nimitta is cause in the most general sense, i.e. what causes existence. The commentator explains it chiefly in a moral sense: Râgâdinimittâbhâvena animittaṃ, tehi ka vimuttan ti animitto vimokho, i.e. owing to the absence of passion and other causes, without causation; because freed from these causes, therefore it is called freedom without causation. See Childers, Pâli Dictionary, p. 270, col. 2, line 1.

The simile is intended to compare the ways of those who have obtained spiritual freedom to the flight of birds, it being difficult to understand how the birds move on without putting their feet on anything. This, at least, is the explanation of the commentator. The same metaphor occurs Mahâbh. XII, 6763. Childers translates, 'leaving no more trace of existence than a bird in the air.'

95. Without the hints given by the commentator, we should probably take the three similes of this verse in their natural sense, as illustrating the imperturbable state of an Arahanta, or venerable person. The earth is always represented as an emblem of patience; the bolt of Indra, if taken in its technical sense, as the bolt of a gate, might likewise suggest the idea of firmness; while the lake is a constant representative of serenity and purity. The commentator, however, suggests that what is meant is, that the earth, though flowers are cast on it, does not feel pleasure, nor a door-step displeasure, although less savoury things are thrown upon it; and that in like manner a wise person is indifferent to honour and dishonour.

96. That this very natural threefold division, thought, word, and deed, the trividha-dvâra or the three doors of the Buddhists (Hardy, Manual, p. 494), was not peculiar to the Buddhists or unknown to the Brâhmans, has been proved against Dr. Weber by Professor Köppen in his 'Religion des Buddha,' I, p. 445. He particularly called attention to Manu XII, 4–8; and he might have added Mahâbh. XII, 4059, 6512, 6549, 6554; XIII, 5677, &c. Dr. Weber has himself afterwards brought forward a passage from the Atharvaveda, VI, 96, 3 (yak kakshushâ manasâ yak ka vâkâ upârima), which, however, has a different meaning. A better one was quoted by him from the Taitt. Âr. X, 1, 12 (yan me manasâ, vâkâ, karmanâ vâ dushkritaṃ kritam). Similar expressions have been shown to exist in the Zendavesta, and among the Manichæans (Lassen, Indische Alterthumskunde, III, p. 414; see also Boehtlingk's Dictionary, s.v. kâya, and Childers, s.v. kâyo). There was no ground, therefore, for supposing that this formula had found its way into the Christian liturgy from Persia, for, as Professor Cowell remarks (Journal of Philology, vol. iii, p. 215), Greek writers, such as Plato, employ very similar expressions, e.g. Protag. p. 348, 30, πρὸς ἅπαν ἔργον καὶ λόγον καὶ διανόημα. In fact, the opposition between words and deeds occurs in almost every writer, from Homer downwards; and the further distinction between thoughts and words is

clearly implied even in such expressions as, 'they say in their heart.' That the idea of sin being committed by thought was not a new idea, even to the Jews, may be seen from Prov. xxiv. 9, 'the thought of foolishness is sin.' In the Âpastamba-sûtras, lately edited by Professor Bühler, we find the expression, atho yatkiñka manasâ vâkâ kakshushâ vâ sankalpayan dhyâyaty âhâbhivipasyati vâ tathaiva tad bhavatîtyupadisanti, 'they say that whatever a Brahman intending with his mind, voice, or eye, thinks, says, or looks, that will be.' This is clearly a very different division, and it is the same which is intended in the passage from the Atharva-veda, quoted above. In the mischief done by the eye, we have, perhaps, the first indication of the evil eye. (Mahâbh. XII, 3417. See Dhammapada, vv. 231–234, and Nâgârguna's Suhrillekha.)

On the technical meaning of tâdi, see Childers, s.v. D'Alwis (p. 78) has evidently received the right interpretation, but has not understood it. Mâdrisa also is used very much like tâdrisa, and from it mâriso, a venerable person, in Sanskrit mârsha.

98. See Childers, s.v. ninnam.

8

The Thousands

100. Even though a speech be a thousand (of words), but made up of senseless words, one word of sense is better, which if a man hears, he becomes quiet.

101. Even though a Gâthâ (poem) be a thousand (of words), but made up of senseless words, one word of a Gâthâ is better, which if a man hears, he becomes quiet.

102. Though a man recite a hundred Gâthâs made up of senseless words, one word of the law is better, which if a man hears, he becomes quiet.

103. If one man conquer in battle a thousand times thousand men, and if another conquer himself, he is the greatest of conquerors.

104, 105. One's own self conquered is better than all other

people; not even a god, a Gandharva, not Mâra with Brahman could change into defeat the victory of a man who has vanquished himself, and always lives under restraint.

106. If a man for a hundred years sacrifice month by month with a thousand, and if he but for one moment pay homage to a man whose soul is grounded (in true knowledge), better is that homage than a sacrifice for a hundred years.

107. If a man for a hundred years worship Agni (fire) in the forest, and if he but for one moment pay homage to a man whose soul is grounded (in true knowledge), better is that homage than sacrifice for a hundred years.

108. Whatever a man sacrifice in this world as an offering or as an oblation for a whole year in order to gain merit, the whole of it is not worth a quarter (a farthing); reverence shown to the righteous is better.

109. He who always greets and constantly reveres the aged, four things will increase to him, viz. life, beauty, happiness, power.

110. But he who lives a hundred years, vicious and unrestrained, a life of one day is better if a man is virtuous and reflecting.

111. And he who lives a hundred years, ignorant and unrestrained, a life of one day is better if a man is wise and reflecting.

112. And he who lives a hundred years, idle and weak, a life of one day is better if a man has attained firm strength.

113. And he who lives a hundred years, not seeing beginning and end, a life of one day is better if a man sees beginning and end.

114. And he who lives a hundred years, not seeing the immortal place, a life of one day is better if a man sees the immortal place.

115. And he who lives a hundred years, not seeing the highest law, a life of one day is better if a man sees the highest law.

---

100. This Sahasravarga, or Chapter of the Thousands, is quoted by that name in the Mahâvastu (Minayeff, Mélanges Asiatiques, VI, p. 583): Teshâm Bhagavâñ gatilânâm Dharmapadeshu sahasravargam bhâshati: 'Sahasram api vâkânâm anarthapadasamhitânâm, ekârthavatî sreyâ yâm srutvâ upasâmyati. Sahasram api gâthânâm anarthapadasamhitânâm, ekârthavatî sreyâ yâm srutvâ upasâmyati' (MS. R. A. S. Lond.) Here the Pâli text seems decidedly more original and perfect.

104. Gitam, according to the commentator, stands for gito (lingavipallâso, i.e. viparyâsa); see also Senart in Journal Asiatique, 1880, p. 500.

The Devas (gods), Gandharvas (fairies), and other fanciful beings of the Brahmanic religion, such as the Nâgas, Sarpas, Garudas, &c., were allowed to continue in the traditional language of the people who had embraced Buddhism. See the pertinent remarks of Burnouf, Introduction, pp. 134 seq., 184. On Mâra, the tempter, see v. 7. Sâstram Aiyar, On the Gaina Religion, p. xx, says: 'Moreover as it is declared in the Gaina Vedas that all the gods worshipped by the various Hindu sects, viz. Siva, Brahma, Vishnu, Ganapati, Subramaniyan, and others, were devoted adherents of the above-mentioned Tîrthankaras, the Gainas therefore do not consider them as unworthy of their worship; but as they are servants of Arugan, they consider them to be deities of their system, and accordingly perform certain pûgâs in honour of them, and worship them also.' The case is more doubtful with orthodox Buddhists.

Orthodox Buddhists,' as Mr. D'Alwis writes (Attanagalu-vansa, p. 55), 'do not consider the worship of the Devas as being sanctioned by him who disclaimed for himself and all the Devas any power over man's soul. Yet the Buddhists are everywhere idol-worshippers. Buddhism, however, acknowledges the existence of some of the Hindu deities, and from the various friendly offices which those Devas are said to have rendered to Gotama, Buddhists evince a respect for their idols.' See also Buddhaghosha's Parables, p. 162.

109. Dr. Fausböll, in a most important note, called attention to the fact that the same verse, with slight variations, occurs in Manu. We there read, II, 121:

*Abhivâdanasîlasya nitya*m vri*ddhopasevinah,*
*Katvâri sampravardhante âyur vidyâ ya*so *balam.*

Here the four things are, life, knowledge, glory, power.

In the Âpastamba-sûtras, I, 2, 5, 15, the reward promised for the same virtue is svargam âyus *ka*, 'heaven and long life.' It seems, therefore, as if the original idea of this verse came from the Brahmans, and was afterwards adopted by the Buddhists. See Mahâbh.V, 1398; Weber, Ind. Stud. XIII, p. 405. How largely it spread is shown by Dr. Fausböll from the Asiatic Researches, XX, p. 259, where the same verse of the Dhammapada is mentioned as being widely in use among the Buddhists of Siam.

112. On kusîto, see note to verse 7.

9

Evil

116. A man should hasten towards the good, and should keep his thought away from evil; if a man does what is good slothfully, his mind delights in evil.

117. If a man commits a sin, let him not do it again; let him not delight in sin: the accumulation of evil is painful.

118. If a man does what is good, let him do it again; let him delight in it: the accumulation of good is delightful.

119. Even an evil-doer sees happiness so long as his evil deed does not ripen; but when his evil deed ripens, then does the evil-doer see evil.

120. Even a good man sees evil days so long as his good deed

does not ripen; but when his good deed ripens, then does the good man see good things.

121. Let no man think lightly of evil, saying in his heart, It will not come nigh unto me. Even by the falling of water-drops a water-pot is filled; the fool becomes full of evil, even if he gather it little by little.

122. Let no man think lightly of good, saying in his heart, It will not come nigh unto me. Even by the falling of water-drops a water-pot is filled; the wise man becomes full of good, even if he gather it little by little.

123. Let a man avoid evil deeds, as a merchant, if he has few companions and carries much wealth, avoids a dangerous road; as a man who loves life avoids poison.

124. He who has no wound on his hand, may touch poison with his hand; poison does not affect one who has no wound; nor is there evil for one who does not commit evil.

125. If a man offend a harmless, pure, and innocent person, the evil falls back upon that fool, like light dust thrown up against the wind.

126. Some people are born again; evil-doers go to hell; righteous people go to heaven; those who are free from all worldly desires attain Nirvâna.

127. Not in the sky, not in the midst of the sea, not if we enter

into the clefts of the mountains, is there known a spot in the whole world where a man might be freed from an evil deed.

128. Not in the sky, not in the midst of the sea, not if we enter into the clefts of the mountains, is there known a spot in the whole world where death could not overcome (the mortal).

---

125. Cf. Suttanipâta, v. 661; Indische Sprüche, 1582; Kathâsaritsâgara, 49, 222.

126. For a description of hell and its long, yet not endless sufferings, see Buddhaghosha's Parables, p. 132. The pleasures of heaven, too, are frequently described in these Parables and elsewhere. Buddha himself enjoyed these pleasures of heaven, before he was born for the last time. It is probably when good and evil deeds are equally balanced, that men are born again as human beings; this, at least, is the opinion of the Gainas. Cf. Chintâmani, ed. H. Bower, Introd. p. xv.

127. Cf. St. Luke xii. 2, 'For there is nothing covered that shall not be revealed;' and Psalm cxxxix. 8–12.

10

Punishment

129. All men tremble at punishment, all men fear death; remember that you are like unto them, and do not kill, nor cause slaughter.

130. All men tremble at punishment, all men love life; remember that thou art like unto them, and do not kill, nor cause slaughter.

131. He who, seeking his own happiness, punishes or kills beings who also long for happiness, will not find happiness after death.

132. He who seeking his own happiness does not punish or kill beings who also long for happiness, will find happiness after death.

133. Do not speak harshly to anybody; those who are spoken to will answer thee in the same way. Angry speech is painful, blows for blows will touch thee.

134. If, like a shattered metal plate (gong), thou utter nothing, then thou hast reached Nirvâna; anger is not known to thee.

135. As a cowherd with his staff drives his cows into the stable, so do Age and Death drive the life of men.

136. A fool does not know when he commits his evil deeds: but the wicked man burns by his own deeds, as if burnt by fire.

137. He who inflicts pain on innocent and harmless persons, will soon come to one of these ten states:

138. He will have cruel suffering, loss, injury of the body, heavy affliction, or loss of mind,

139. Or a misfortune coming from the king, or a fearful accusation, or loss of relations, or destruction of treasures,

140. Or lightning-fire will burn his houses; and when his body is destroyed, the fool will go to hell.

141. Not nakedness, not platted hair, not dirt, not fasting, or lying on the earth, not rubbing with dust, not sitting motionless, can purify a mortal who has not overcome desires.

142. He who, though dressed in fine apparel, exercises tranquillity, is quiet, subdued, restrained, chaste, and has ceased to find fault with all other beings, he indeed is a Brâhmana, an ascetic (sramana), a friar (bhikshu).

143. Is there in this world any man so restrained by shame that he does not provoke reproof, as a noble horse the whip?

144. Like a noble horse when touched by the whip, be ye strenuous and eager, and by faith, by virtue, by energy, by meditation, by discernment of the law you will overcome this great pain, perfect in knowledge and in behaviour, and never forgetful.

145. Well-makers lead the water (wherever they like); fletchers bend the arrow; carpenters bend a log of wood; good people fashion themselves.

---

129. One feels tempted, no doubt, to take upama in the sense of 'the nearest (der Nächste), the neighbour,' and to translate, 'having made oneself one's neighbour,' i.e. loving one's neighbour as oneself. But as upamăm, with a short a, is the correct accusative of upamâ, we must translate, 'having made oneself the likeness, the image of others, having placed oneself in the place of others.' This is an expression which occurs frequently in Sanskrit; cf. Hitopadeśa I, 11:

Prânâ yathâtmano ʂo bhîshtâ bhûtânâm api te tathâ,
Âtmaupamyena bhûteshu dayâm kurvanti sâdhavah.

'As life is dear to oneself, it is dear also to other living beings: by comparing oneself with others, good people bestow pity on all beings.'
See also Hit. I, 12; Râm. V, 23, 5, âtmânam upamâm kritvâ sveshu dâreshu ramyatâm, 'making oneself a likeness, i.e. putting oneself in the position of other people, it is right to love none but one's own wife.' Dr. Fausböll has called attention to similar passages in the Mahâbhârata, XIII, 5569 seq.
130. Cf. St. Luke vi. 31.
131. Dr. Fausböll points out the striking similarity between this verse and two verses occurring in Manu and the Mahâbhârata:—Manu V, 45:
Yo x himsakâni bhûtâni hinasty âtmasukhekkhayâ,
Sa ǵivaṃs ka mritas kaiva na kvakit sukham edhate. Mahâbhârata XIII, 5568:
Ahiṃsakâni bhûtâni daṇḍena vinihanti yah,
Âtmanah sukham ikkhan sa pretya naiva sukhî bhavet. If it were not for

· 89 ·

ahimsakâni, in which Manu and the Mahâbhârata agree, I should say that the verses in both were Sanskrit modifications of the Pâli original. The verse in the Mahâbhârata presupposes the verse of the Dhammapada.

133. See Mahâbhârata XII, 4056.

134. See Childers, s.v. nibbâna, p. 270, and s.v. kâmso; D'Alwis, Buddhist Nirvâna, p. 35.

136. The metaphor of 'burning' for 'suffering' is very common in Buddhist literature. Everything burns, i.e. everything suffers, was one of the first experiences of Buddha himself. See v. 146.

138. 'Cruel suffering' is explained by sîsaroga, 'headache,' &c. 'Loss' is taken for loss of money. 'Injury of the body' is held to be the cutting off of the arm, and other limbs. 'Heavy afflictions' are, again, various kinds of diseases.

139. Upasarga means 'accident, misfortune.' Dr. Fausböll translates râgato va upassaggam by 'fulgentis (lunae) defectionem;' Dr. Weber by 'Bestrafung vom König;' Beal by 'some governmental difficulty.' Abbhakkhânam, Sanskrit abhyâkhyânam, is a heavy accusation for high treason, or similar offences. Beal translates, 'some false accusation.' The 'destruction of pleasures or treasures' is explained by gold being changed to coals (see Buddhaghosha's Parables, p. 98; Thiessen, Kisâgotamî, p. 6), pearls to cotton seed, corn to potsherds, and by men and cattle becoming blind, lame, &c.

141. Cf. Hibbert Lectures, p. 355. Dr. Fausböll has pointed out that the same or a very similar verse occurs in a legend taken from the Divyâvadâna, and translated by Burnouf (Introduction, p. 313 seq.) Burnouf translates the verse: 'Ce n'est ni la coutume de marcher nu, ni les cheveux nattés, ni l'usage d'argile, ni le choix des diverses espèces d'aliments, ni l'habitude de coucher sur la terre nue, ni la poussière, ni la malpropreté, ni l'attention à fuir l'abri d'un toit, qui sont capables de dissiper le trouble dans lequel nous jettent les désirs non-satisfaits; mais qu'un homme, maître de ses sens, calme, recueilli, chaste, évitant de faire du mal à aucune créature, accomplisse la Loi, et il sera, quoique paré d'ornements, un Brâhmane, un Çramana, un Religieux.' See also Suttanipâta, v. 248.

Walking naked and the other things mentioned in our verse are outward signs of a saintly life, and these Buddha rejects because they do not calm the passions. Nakedness he seems to have rejected on other grounds too, if we may judge from the Sumâgadhâ-avadâna: 'A number of naked friars were assembled in the house of the daughter of Anâtha-pindika. She called her daughter-in-law, Sumâgadhâ, and said, "Go and see those highly respectable persons." Sumâgadhâ, expecting to see some of the saints, like Sâriputra, Maudgalyâyana, and others, ran out full of joy. But when she saw these friars with their hair like pigeon wings, covered by nothing but dirt, offensive, and looking like demons, she became sad. "Why are you sad?" said her mother-in-law. Sumâgadhâ replied, "O mother, if these are saints, what must sinners be like?'"

Burnouf (Introduction, p. 312) supposed that the Gainas only, and not the Buddhists, allowed nakedness. But the Gainas, too, do not allow it universally. They are divided into two parties, the Svetambaras and Digambaras. The Svetambaras, clad in white, are the followers of Parsvanâtha, and wear clothes. The Digambaras, i.e. sky-clad, disrobed, are followers of Mahâvîra, resident chiefly in Southern India. At present they, too, wear clothing, but not when eating. See Sâstram Aiyar, p. xxi.

The gatâ, or the hair platted and gathered up in a knot, was a sign of a Saiva ascetic. The sitting motionless is one of the postures assumed by ascetics. Clough explains ukkutika as 'the act of sitting on the heels;' Wilson gives for utkatukâsana, 'sitting on the hams.' See Fausböll, note on verse 140.

142. This verse has to be taken in connection with the preceding verse, to show that though a man cares about his outward appearance and is well dressed, he may be a true disciple for all that, if only he practises virtue. As to dandanidhâna, see Mahâbh. XII, 6559, and Suttanipâta, v. 34.

145. The same as verse 80. According to Fausböll and Subhûti we ought to render the verses by, 'What man is there found on earth so restrained by shame that he never provokes reproof, as a good horse the whip?' See, however, Childers, s.v. appabodhati. Fausböll maintains his view.

11

Old Age

146. How is there laughter, how is there joy, as this world is always burning? Do you not seek a light, ye who are surrounded by darkness?

147. Look at this dressed-up lump, covered with wounds, joined together, sickly, full of many schemes, but which has no strength, no hold!

148. This body is wasted, full of sickness, and frail; this heap of corruption breaks to pieces, life indeed ends in death.

149. After one has looked at those grey bones, thrown away like gourds in the autumn, what pleasure is there (left in life)!

150. After a stronghold has been made of the bones, it is covered

with flesh and blood, and there dwell in it old age and death, pride and deceit.

151. The brilliant chariots of kings are destroyed, the body also approaches destruction, but the virtue of good people never approaches destruction,—thus do the good say to the good.

152. A man who has learnt little, grows old like an ox; his flesh grows, but his knowledge does not grow.

153, 154. Looking for the maker of this tabernacle, I have run through a course of many births, not finding him; and painful is birth again and again. But now, maker of the tabernacle, thou hast been seen; thou shalt not make up this tabernacle again. All thy rafters are broken, thy ridge-pole is sundered; the mind, approaching the Eternal (visankhâra, nirvâna), has attained to the extinction of all desires.

155. Men who have not observed proper discipline, and have not gained wealth in their youth, perish like old herons in a lake without fish.

156. Men who have not observed proper discipline, and have not gained wealth in their youth, lie, like broken bows, sighing after the past.

---

148. Dr. Fausböll informs me that Childers proposed the emendation ma-ranantam hi ǵivitam. The following extract from a letter, addressed by Childers to Dr. Fausböll, will be read with interest:—'As regards Dhp. v. 148, I have no doubt whatever. I quite agree with you that the idea (mors est vita ejus) is a profound

and noble one, but the question is, Is the idea there? I think not. Mara*nam* tamhi ĝîvita*m* is not Pâli, I mean not a Pâli construction, and years ago even it grated on my ear as a harsh phrase. The reading of your MSS. of the texts is nothing; your MSS. of Dhammapada are very bad ones, and it is merely the vicious Sinhalese spelling of bad MSS., like kamma*mtam* for kammanta*m*. But the comment sets the question at rest at once, for it explains mara*nant*am by mara*nap*ariyosâna*m*, which is exactly the same. I see there is one serious difficulty left, that all your MSS. seem to have tamhi, and not ta*m* hi; but are you sure it is so? There was a Dhammapada in the India Office Library, and I had a great hunt for it a few days ago, but to my deep disappointment it is missing. I do not agree with you that the sentence "All Life is bounded by Death," is trivial: it is a truism, but half the noblest passages in poetry are truisms, and unless I greatly mistake, this very passage will be found in many other literatures.'

Dr. Fausböll adds:—

'I have still the same doubt as before, because of all my MSS. reading mara*nam* tamhi. I do not know the readings of the London MSS. The explanation of the commentary does not settle the question, as it may as well be considered an explanation of my reading as of the reading which Childers proposed.—v. FAUSBÖLL.'

Fausböll has now surrendered his doubts, and he produces himself a number of passages where this phrase mara*nânt*am hi ĝîvanam occurs, e.g. Mahâbh. (ed. Calcutta), XI, 48; 207; XII, 829; Râmây. (ed. Bombay), Ayodhyâk., p. 197; Divyâvadâna, p. 27; 100.

149. In the Rudrâya*nâ*vadâna of the Divyâvadâna this verse appears as,

Yânîmâny apariddhâni vikshiptâni diso disah,
Kapotavarnâny asthîni tâni drishtvaiha kâ ratíh.

See Schiefner, Mél. Asiat. VIII, p. 589; Gâtaka, vol. i, p. 322.

150. The expression ma*m*salohitalepanam is curiously like the expression used in Manu VI, 76, ma*m*salohitalepanam, and in several passages of the Mahâbhârata, XII, 12462, 12053, as pointed out by Dr. Fausböll.

153, 154. These two verses are famous among Buddhists, for they are the words which the founder of Buddhism is supposed to have uttered at the moment he attained to Buddhahood. (See Spence Hardy, Manual, p. 180.) According to the Lalita-vistara, however, the words uttered on that solemn occasion were those quoted in the note to verse 39. In the commentary on the Brahmagâla this verse is called the first speech of Buddha, his last speech being the words in the Mahâparinibbâna-sutta, 'Life is subject to age; strive in earnest, &c.' The words used in the Mahâparinibbâna-sutta, Chap. IV, 2, *Katunnam* dhammânam ananubodhâ appativedhâ evam idam dîgham addhânam sandhâvitam samsâritam mamañ k' eva tumhâkañ ka, answer to the anticipation expressed in our verse.

The exact rendering of this verse has been much discussed, chiefly by Mr. D'Alwis in the Attanugaluvansa, p. cxxviii, and again in his Buddhist Nirvâna, p. 78; also by Childers, Notes on Dhammapada, p. 4, and in his Dictionary. Gogerly translated: 'Through various transmigrations I must travel, if I do not discover the builder whom I seek.' Spence Hardy: 'Through many different births I have run (to me not having found), seeking the architect of the desire-resembling house.' Fausböll: 'Multiplices generationis revolutiones percurreram, non inveniens, domus (corporis) fabricatorem quaerens.' And again (p. 322): 'Multarum generationum revolutio mihi subeunda esset, nisi invenissem domus fabricatorem.' Childers: 'I have run through the revolution of countless births, seeking the architect of this dwelling and finding him not.' D'Alwis: 'Through transmigrations of numerous births have I run, not discovering, (though) seeking the house-builder.' All depends on how we take sandhavissam, which Fausböll takes as a conditional, Childers, following Trenckner, as an aorist, because the sense imperatively requires an aorist. I had formerly translated it as a future, though qualifying it by the participle present anibbisan, i.e. not finding, and taking it in the sense of, if or so long as I do not find the true cause of existence. Anibbisan I had translated by not resting (anirvisan), but the commentator seems to authorise the meaning of not finding (avindanto, alabhanto), and in that case all the material difficulties of the verse seem to me to disappear.

'The maker of the tabernacle' is explained as a poetical expression for the cause of new births, at least according to the views of Buddha's followers, whatever his own views may have been. Buddha had conquered Mâra, the representative of worldly temptations, the father of worldly desires, and as desires (tamhâ) are, by means of upâdâna and bhava, the cause of gâti, or 'birth,' the destruction of desires and the conquest of Mâra are nearly the same thing, though expressed differently in the philosophical and legendary language of the Buddhists. Tamhâ, 'thirst' or 'craving,' is mentioned as serving in the army of Mâra. (Lotus, p. 443.)

155. On ghâyanti, i.e. kshâyanti, see Dr. Bollensen's learned remarks, Zeitschrift der Deutschen Morgenl. Gesellschaft, XVIII, 834, and Boehtlingk-Roth, s.v. kshâ.

12

Self

157. If a man hold himself dear, let him watch himself carefully; during one at least out of the three watches a wise man should be watchful.

158. Let each man direct himself first to what is proper, then let him teach others; thus a wise man will not suffer.

159. If a man make himself as he teaches others to be, then, being himself well subdued, he may subdue (others); for one's own self is difficult to subdue.

160. Self is the lord of self, who else could be the lord? With self well subdued, a man finds a lord such as few can find.

161. The evil done by oneself, self-begotten, self-bred, crushes the foolish, as a diamond breaks even a precious stone.

162. He whose wickedness is very great brings himself down to that state where his enemy wishes him to be, as a creeper does with the tree which it surrounds.

163. Bad deeds, and deeds hurtful to ourselves, are easy to do; what is beneficial and good, that is very difficult to do.

164. The foolish man who scorns the rule of the venerable (Arahat), of the elect (Ariya), of the virtuous, and follows a false doctrine, he bears fruit to his own destruction, like the fruits of the Katthaka reed.

165. By oneself the evil is done, by oneself one suffers; by oneself evil is left undone, by oneself one is purified. The pure and the impure (stand and fall) by themselves, no one can purify another.

166. Let no one forget his own duty for the sake of another's, however great; let a man, after he has discerned his own duty, be always attentive to his duty.

---

157. The three watches of the night are meant for the three stages of life. Cf. St. Mark xiii. 37, 'And what I say unto you, I say unto all, Watch.'

158. Cf. Gâtaka, vol. ii, p. 441.

161. The Chinese translation renders vagiram by 'steel drill.'

164. The reed either dies after it has borne fruit, or is cut down for the sake of its fruit.

Ditthi, literally 'view,' is used even by itself, like the Greek 'hairesis,' in the sense of heresy (see Burnouf, Lotus, p. 444). In other places a distinction is made between mikkhâditthi (vv. 167, 316) and sammâditthi (v. 319). If arahatam ariyânam are used in their technical sense, we should translate 'the reverend Arhats,'—Arhat being the highest degree of the four orders of Ariyas, viz. Srotaâpanna, Sakadâgâmin, Anâgâmin, and Arhat. See note to verse 178.

166. Attha, lit. 'object,' must here be taken in a moral sense, as 'duty' rather

than as 'advantage.' Childers rendered it by 'spiritual good.' The story which Buddhaghosa tells of the Thera Attadattha gives a clue to the origin of some of his parables, which seem to have been invented to suit the text of the Dhammapada rather than vice versâ. A similar case occurs in the commentary to verse 227.

13

The World

167. Do not follow the evil law! Do not live on in thoughtlessness! Do not follow false doctrine! Be not a friend of the world.

168. Rouse thyself! do not be idle! Follow the law of virtue! The virtuous rests in bliss in this world and in the next.

169. Follow the law of virtue; do not follow that of sin. The virtuous rests in bliss in this world and in the next.

170. Look upon the world as you would on a bubble, look upon it as you would on a mirage: the king of death does not see him who thus looks down upon the world.

171. Come, look at this world, glittering like a royal chariot; the foolish are immersed in it, but the wise do not touch it.

172. He who formerly was reckless and afterwards became sober, brightens up this world, like the moon when freed from clouds.

173. He whose evil deeds are covered by good deeds, brightens up this world, like the moon when freed from clouds.

174. This world is dark, few only can see here; a few only go to heaven, like birds escaped from the net.

175. The swans go on the path of the sun, they go miraculously through the ether; the wise are led out of this world, when they have conquered Mâra and his train.

176. If a man has transgressed the one law, and speaks lies, and scoffs at another world, there is no evil he will not do.

177. The uncharitable do not go to the world of the gods; fools only do not praise liberality; a wise man rejoices in liberality, and through it becomes blessed in the other world.

178. Better than sovereignty over the earth, better than going to heaven, better than lordship over all worlds, is the reward of Sotâpatti, the first step in holiness.

---

167. Childers says, I have not the slightest notion of the meaning of loka-vaddhano. Could it mean, Do not swell the number of worldlings?

168, 169. See Rhys Davids, Buddhism, p. 65.

170. See Suttanipâta, v. 1118.

175. Hamsa may be meant for the bird, whether flamingo, or swan, or ibis (see Hardy, Manual, p. 17), but it may also, I believe, be taken in the sense of saint. As to iddhi, 'magical power,' i.e. riddhi, see Burnouf, Lotus, p. 310; Spence Hardy, Manual, pp. 498, 504; Legends, pp. 55, 177; and note to verse 254.

178. Sotâpatti, the technical term for the first step in the path that leads to Nirvâna. There are four such steps, or stages, and on entering each, a man receives a new title:—

(1) The Srotaâpanna, lit. he who has got into the stream. A man may have seven more births before he reaches the other shore, i.e. Nirvâna.

(2) Sakridâgâmin, lit. he who comes back once, so called because, after having entered this stage, a man is born only once more among men or gods. Childers shows that this involves really two more births, one in the deva world, the other in the world of men. Burnouf says the same, Introduction, p. 293.

(3) Anâgâmin, lit. he who does not come back, so called because, after this stage, a man cannot be born again in a lower world, but can only be born into a Brahman world, before he reaches Nirvâna.

(4) Arhat, the venerable, the perfect, who has reached the highest stage that can be reached, and from which Nirvâna is perceived (sukkhavipassanâ, Lotus, p. 849). See Hardy, Eastern Monachism, p. 280; Burnouf, Introduction, p. 209; Köppen, p. 398; D'Alwis, Attanugaluvansa, p. cxxiv; Feer, Sutra en 42 articles, p. 6.

14

The Buddha (the Awakened)

179. He whose conquest cannot be conquered again, into whose conquest no one in this world enters, by what track can you lead him, the Awakened, the Omniscient, the trackless?

180. He whom no desire with its snares and poisons can lead astray, by what track can you lead him, the Awakened, the Omniscient, the trackless?

181. Even the gods envy those who are awakened and not forgetful, who are given to meditation, who are wise, and who delight in the repose of retirement (from the world).

182. Difficult (to obtain) is the conception of men, difficult is the life of mortals, difficult is the hearing of the True Law, difficult is the birth of the Awakened (the attainment of Buddhahood).

183. Not to commit any sin, to do good, and to purify one's mind, that is the teaching of (all) the Awakened.

184. The Awakened call patience the highest penance, long-suffering the highest Nirvâna; for he is not an anchorite (pravragita) who strikes others, he is not an ascetic (sramana) who insults others.

185. Not to blame, not to strike, to live restrained under the law, to be moderate in eating, to sleep and sit alone, and to dwell on the highest thoughts,—this is the teaching of the Awakened.

186. There is no satisfying lusts, even by a shower of gold pieces; he who knows that lusts have a short taste and cause pain, he is wise;

187. Even in heavenly pleasures he finds no satisfaction, the disciple who is fully awakened delights only in the destruction of all desires.

188. Men, driven by fear, go to many a refuge, to mountains and forests, to groves and sacred trees.

189. But that is not a safe refuge, that is not the best refuge; a man is not delivered from all pains after having gone to that refuge.

190. He who takes refuge with Buddha, the Law, and the Church; he who, with clear understanding, sees the four holy truths:—

191. Viz. pain, the origin of pain, the destruction of pain, and the eightfold holy way that leads to the quieting of pain;—

192. That is the safe refuge, that is the best refuge; having gone to that refuge, a man is delivered from all pain.

193. A supernatural person (a Buddha) is not easily found, he is not born everywhere. Wherever such a sage is born, that race prospers.

194. Happy is the arising of the awakened, happy is the teaching of the True Law, happy is peace in the church, happy is the devotion of those who are at peace.

195, 196. He who pays homage to those who deserve homage, whether the awakened (Buddha) or their disciples, those who have overcome the host (of evils), and crossed the flood of sorrow, he who pays homage to such as have found deliverance and know no fear, his merit can never be measured by anybody.

179, 180. Buddha, the Awakened, is to be taken as an appellative rather than as the proper name of the Buddha (see v. 183). It means, anybody who has arrived at complete knowledge. Anantagokaram I take in the sense of, possessed of unlimited knowledge. Apadam, which Dr. Fausböll takes as an epithet of Buddha and translates by 'non investigabilis,' is translated 'trackless,' in order to show the play on the word pada; see Childers, s.v. The commentator says: 'The man who is possessed of even a single one of such conditions as râga, &c., him ye may lead forward; but the Buddha has not even one condition or basis of renewed existence, and therefore by what track will you lead this unconditioned Buddha?' Cf. Dhp. vv. 92, 420; and Gâtaka, vol. i, pp. 79, 313.

182. Mr. Beal (Dhammapada, p. 110) states that this verse occurs also in the Sûtra of the forty-two sections.

183. This verse is again one of the most solemn verses among the Buddhists. According to Csoma Körösi, it ought to follow the famous Âryâ stanza, 'Ye dhammâ' (Lotus, p. 522), and serve as its complement. But though this may be the case in Tibet, it was not so originally. The same verse (ascribed to Kanakamuni) occurs at the end of the Chinese translation of the Prâtimoksha (Beal, J. R. A. S. XIX, p. 473; Catena, p. 159); in the Tibetan translation of the Gâthâsangraha, v. 14 (Schiefner, Mél. Asiat. VIII, pp. 568, 586; and Csoma Körösi, As. Res. XX, p. 79). Burnouf has fully discussed the metre and meaning of our verse on pp. 527, 528 of his 'Lotus.' He prefers sakittaparidamanam, which Csoma translated by 'the mind must be brought under entire subjection' (svakittaparidamanam), and the late Dr. Mill by 'proprii intellects subjugatio.' But his own MS. of the Mahâpadhâna-sutta gave likewise sakittapariyodapanam, and this is no doubt the correct reading. (See D'Alwis, Attanugaluvansa, p. cxxix.) We found pariyodapeyya in verse 88, in the sense of purging oneself from the troubles of the mind. From the same verb, (pari) ava + dai, we may derive the name Avadâna, a legend, originally a pure and virtuous act, an ἀρίστεια, afterwards a sacred story, and possibly a story the hearing of which purifies the mind. See Boehtlingk-Roth, s.v. avadâna.

184. Childers, following the commentator, translates, 'Patience, which is long-suffering, is the best devotion, the Buddhas declare that Nirvâna is the best (of things).'

185. Pâtimokkhe, 'under the law,' i.e. according to the law, the law which leads to Moksha, or 'freedom.' Prâtimoksha is the title of the oldest collection of the moral laws of the Buddhists (Burnouf, Introduction, p. 300; Bigandet, The Life of Gaudama, p. 439; Rhys Davids, Buddhism, p. 162), and as it was common both to the Southern and the Northern Buddhists, pâtimokkhe in our passage may possibly be meant, as Professor Weber suggests, as the title of that very collection. The commentator explains it by getthakasîla and pâtimokkhasîla. Sayanâsam might stand for sayanâsanam, see Mahâbh. XII, 6684; but in Buddhist literature it is intended for sayanâsanam, see also Mahâbh. XII, 9978, sayyâsane. Fausböll now reads pântam instead of patthañ, as in Suttanipâta, 337.

187. There is a curious similarity between this verse and verse 6503 (9919) of the Sântiparva:

Yakka kâmasukham loke, yak ka divyam mahat sukham,
Trishnâkshayasukhasyaite nârhatah shodasîm kalâm.

'And whatever delight of love there is on earth, and whatever is the great delight in heaven, they are not worth the sixteenth part of the pleasure which springs from the destruction of all desires.' The two verses 186, 187 are ascribed to king Mandhâtri, shortly before his death (Mél. Asiat. VIII, p. 471; see also Gâtaka, vol. ii, p. 113).

188–192. These verses occur in Sanskrit in the Prâtihâryasûtra, translated by Burnouf, Introduction, pp. 162–189; see p. 186. Burnouf translates rukkhaketyâni by 'arbres consacrés;' properly, sacred shrines under or near a tree. See also Gâtaka, vol. i, p. 97.

190. Buddha, Dharma, and Sangha are called the Trisarana (cf. Burnouf, Introd. p. 630). The four holy truths are the four statements that there is pain in this world, that the source of pain is desire, that desire can be annihilated, that there is a way (shown by Buddha) by which the annihilation of all desires can be achieved, and freedom be obtained. That way consists of eight parts. (See Burnouf, Introduction, p. 630.) The eightfold way forms the subject of Chapter XVIII. (See also Feer, Journal As. 1870, p. 418, and Chips from a German Workshop, 2nd ed. vol. i, p. 251 seq.)

15

Happiness

197. We live happily indeed, not hating those who hate us! among men who hate us we dwell free from hatred!

198. We live happily indeed, free from ailments among the ailing! among men who are ailing let us dwell free from ailments!

199. We live happily indeed, free from greed among the greedy! among men who are greedy let us dwell free from greed!

200. We live happily indeed, though we call nothing our own! We shall be like the bright gods, feeding on happiness!

201. Victory breeds hatred, for the conquered is unhappy. He who has given up both victory and defeat, he, the contented, is happy.

202. There is no fire like passion; there is no losing throw like

hatred; there is no pain like this body; there is no happiness higher than rest.

203. Hunger is the worst of diseases, the elements of the body the greatest evil; if one knows this truly, that is Nirvâna, the highest happiness.

204. Health is the greatest of gifts, contentedness the best riches; trust is the best of relationships, Nirvâna the highest happiness.

205. He who has tasted the sweetness of solitude and tranquillity, is free from fear and free from sin, while he tastes the sweetness of drinking in the law.

206. The sight of the elect (Arya) is good, to live with them is always happiness; if a man does not see fools, he will be truly happy.

207. He who walks in the company of fools suffers a long way; company with fools, as with an enemy, is always painful; company with the wise is pleasure, like meeting with kinsfolk.

208. Therefore, one ought to follow the wise, the intelligent, the learned, the much enduring, the dutiful, the elect; one ought to follow such a good and wise man, as the moon follows the path of the stars.

---

198. The ailment here meant is moral rather than physical. Cf. Mahâbh. XII, 9924, samprasânto nirâmayah; 9925, yo x sau prânântiko rogas tâm trishnâm tyagatah sukham.

200. The words placed in the mouth of the king of Videha, while his residence Mithilâ was in flames, are curiously like our verse; cf. Mahâbh. XII, 9917,

Susukham vata gîvâmi yasya me nâsti kiñkana,
Mithilâyâm pradîptâyâm na me dahyati kiñkana.

'I live happily, indeed, for I have nothing; while Mithilâ is in flames, nothing of mine is burning.' Cf. Muir, Religious Sentiments, p. 106.

The âbhassara, i.e. âbhâsvara, 'the bright gods,' are frequently mentioned. Cf. Burnouf, Introd. p. 611.

201. This verse is ascribed to Buddha, when he heard of the defeat of Agâtasatru by Prasenagit. It exists in the Northern or Sanskrit and in the Southern or Pâli texts, i.e. in the Avadânasataka, in the Samyutta-nikâya. See Feer, Comptes Rendus, 1871, p. 44, and Journal As. 1880, p. 509. In the Avadâna-sataka, the Sanskrit version is—

Gayo vairam prasavati, duhkham sete parâgitah,
Upasântah sukham sete hitvâ gayaparâgayam.

202. I take kali in the sense of an unlucky die which makes a player lose his game. A real simile seems wanted here, as in verse 251, where, for the same reason, I translate graha by 'shark,' not by 'captivitas,' as Dr. Fausböll proposes. The same scholar translates kali in our verse by 'peccatum.' If there is any objection to translating kali in Pâli by 'unlucky die,' I should still prefer to take it in the sense of the age of depravity, or the demon of depravity. To judge from Abhidhânappadîpikâ, 1106, kali was used for parâgaya, i.e. loss at game, a losing throw, and occurs in that sense again in verse 252. The Chinese translation has, 'there is no distress (poison) worse than hate.' A similar verse occurs Mahâbh. Sântip. 175, v. 35.

'Body' for khandha is a free translation, but it is difficult to find any better rendering. The Chinese translation also has 'body.' According to the Buddhists each sentient being consists of five khandhas (skandha), or aggregates, the organized body (rûpakhandha) with its four internal capacities of sensation (vedanâ), perception (sañgñâ), conception (samskâra), knowledge (vigñâna). See Burnouf, Introd. pp. 589, 634; Lotus, p. 335.

203. Samskâra is the fourth of the five khandhas, but the commentator takes it here, as well as in verse 255, for the five khandhas together, in which case we can only translate it by 'body,' or 'elements of the body.' See also verse 278. Childers proposes 'organic life' (Notes on Dhammapada, p. 1). There are, however, other samskâras, which follow immediately upon avidyâ, 'ignorance,' as second in the series of the nidânas, or 'causes of existence,' and these too might be called the greatest pain, considering that they are the cause of birth, which is the cause of all pain. Sometimes, again, samskâra seems to have a different and

less technical meaning, being used in the sense of conceptions, plans, desires, as, for instance, in verse 368, where saṅkhârânam khayam is used much like tamhâkhaya. Again, in his comment on verse 75, Buddhaghosa says, upadhiviveko saṅkhârasaṅganikam vinodeti; and again, upadhiviveko ka nirupadhînâm puggalânam visaṅkhâra gatânâm.

For a similar sentiment, see Stanislas Julien, Les Avadânas, vol. i, p. 40, 'Le corps est la plus grande source de souffrance,' &c. I should say that the khandhas in verse 202 and the saṅkhâras in verse 203 are nearly, if not quite, synonymous. I should prefer to read gigakkhâ-paramâ as a compound. Gigakkhâ, or as it is written in one MS., digakkhâ (Sk. gighatsâ), means not only 'hunger,' but 'appetite, desire.'

204. Childers translates, 'the best kinsman is a man you can trust.'

205. Cf. Suttanipâta, v. 256.

207. I should like to read sukho ka dhîrasamvâso.

16

Pleasure

209. He who gives himself to vanity, and does not give himself to meditation, forgetting the real aim (of life) and grasping at pleasure, will in time envy him who has exerted himself in meditation.

210. Let no man ever cling to what is pleasant, or to what is unpleasant. Not to see what is pleasant is pain, and it is pain to see what is unpleasant.

211. Let, therefore, no man love anything; loss of the beloved is evil. Those who love nothing, and hate nothing, have no fetters.

212. From pleasure comes grief, from pleasure comes fear; he who is free from pleasure knows neither grief nor fear.

213. From affection comes grief, from affection comes fear; he who is free from affection knows neither grief nor fear.

214. From lust comes grief, from lust comes fear; he who is free from lust knows neither grief nor fear.

215. From love comes grief, from love comes fear; he who is free from love knows neither grief nor fear.

216. From greed comes grief, from greed comes fear; he who is free from greed knows neither grief nor fear.

217. He who possesses virtue and intelligence, who is just, speaks the truth, and does what is his own business, him the world will hold dear.

218. He in whom a desire for the Ineffable (Nirvâna) has sprung up, who in his mind is satisfied, and whose thoughts are not bewildered by love, he is called ûrdhvaṃsrotas (carried upwards by the stream).

219. Kinsmen, friends, and lovers salute a man who has been long away, and returns safe from afar.

220. In like manner his good works receive him who has done good, and has gone from this world to the other;—as kinsmen receive a friend on his return.

---

214. See Beal, Catena, p. 200.

218. Ûrdhvaṃsrotas or uddhaṃsoto is the technical name for one who has

reached the world of the Avríhas (Aviha), and is proceeding to that of the Akan-ishthas (Akanittha). This is the last stage before he reaches the formless world, the Arûpadhâtu. (See Buddhaghosha's Parables, p. 123; Burnouf, Introduction, p. 599.) Originally ûrdhvamsrotas may have been used in a less technical sense, meaning one who swims against the stream, and is not carried away by the vulgar passions of the world.

17

Anger

221. Let a man leave anger, let him forsake pride, let him overcome all bondage! No sufferings befall the man who is not attached to name and form, and who calls nothing his own.

222. He who holds back rising anger like a rolling chariot, him I call a real driver; other people are but holding the reins.

223. Let a man overcome anger by love, let him overcome evil by good; let him overcome the greedy by liberality, the liar by truth!

224. Speak the truth, do not yield to anger; give, if thou art asked for little; by these three steps thou wilt go near the gods.

225. The sages who injure nobody, and who always control their

body, they will go to the unchangeable place (Nirvâna), where, if they have gone, they will suffer no more.

226. Those who are ever watchful, who study day and night, and who strive after Nirvâna, their passions will come to an end.

227. This is an old saying, O Atula, this is not as if of to-day: 'They blame him who sits silent, they blame him who speaks much, they also blame him who says little; there is no one on earth who is not blamed.'

228. There never was, there never will be, nor is there now, a man who is always blamed, or a man who is always praised.

229, 230. But he whom those who discriminate praise continually day after day, as without blemish, wise, rich in knowledge and virtue, who would dare to blame him, like a coin made of gold from the Gambû river? Even the gods praise him, he is praised even by Brahman.

231. Beware of bodily anger, and control thy body! Leave the sins of the body, and with thy body practise virtue!

232. Beware of the anger of the tongue, and control thy tongue! Leave the sins of the tongue, and practise virtue with thy tongue!

233. Beware of the anger of the mind, and control thy mind! Leave the sins of the mind, and practise virtue with thy mind!

234. The wise who control their body, who control their tongue, the wise who control their mind, are indeed well controlled.

---

221. 'Name and form' is the translation of nâma-rûpa, the ninth of the Buddhist Nidânas. It comprises everything in the phenomenal world. Cf. Burnouf, Introduction, p. 501; see also Gogerly, Lecture on Buddhism, and Bigandet, The Life of Gaudama, p. 454.

223. Mahâbh. XII, 3550, asâdhum sadhunâ gayet. Cf. Ten Gâtakas, ed. Fausböll, p. 5.

227. It appears from the commentary that porânam and aggatanam are neuters, referring to what happened formerly and what happens to-day, and that they are not to be taken as adjectives referring to âsînam, &c. The commentator must have read atula instead of atulam, and he explains it as the name of a pupil whom Gautama addressed by that name (see note to verse 166). Others take atula in the sense of incomparable (Mahâbh. XIII, 1937), and in that case we ought to supply, with Professor Weber, some such word as 'saw' or 'saying.'

230. The Brahman Worlds are higher than the Deva worlds as the Brahman is higher than a Deva; see Hardy, Manual, p. 25; Burnouf, Introduction, pp. 134, 184.

18

Impurity

235. Thou art now like a sear leaf, the messengers of death (Yama) have come near to thee; thou standest at the door of thy departure, and thou hast no provision for thy journey.

236. Make thyself an island, work hard, be wise! When thy impurities are blown away, and thou art free from guilt, thou wilt enter into the heavenly world of the elect (Ariya).

237. Thy life has come to an end, thou art come near to death (Yama), there is no resting-place for thee on the road, and thou hast no provision for thy journey.

238. Make thyself an island, work hard, be wise! When thy impurities are blown away, and thou art free from guilt, thou wilt not enter again into birth and decay.

239. Let a wise man blow off the impurities of himself, as a smith blows off the impurities of silver, one by one, little by little, and from time to time.

240. As the impurity which springs from the iron, when it springs from it, destroys it; thus do a transgressor's own works lead him to the evil path.

241. The taint of prayers is non-repetition; the taint of houses, non-repair; the taint of complexion is sloth; the taint of a watch-man, thoughtlessness.

242. Bad conduct is the taint of woman, niggardliness the taint of a benefactor; tainted are all evil ways, in this world and in the next.

243. But there is a taint worse than all taints,—ignorance is the greatest taint. O mendicants! throw off that taint, and become taintless!

244. Life is easy to live for a man who is without shame, a crow hero, a mischief-maker, an insulting, bold, and wretched fellow.

245. But life is hard to live for a modest man, who always looks for what is pure, who is disinterested, quiet, spotless, and intelligent.

246. He who destroys life, who speaks untruth, who in the world takes what is not given him, who goes to another man's wife;

247. And the man who gives himself to drinking intoxicating liquors, he, even in this world, digs up his own root.

248. O man, know this, that the unrestrained are in a bad state; take care that greediness and vice do not bring thee to grief for a long time!

249. The world gives according to their faith or according to their pleasure: if a man frets about the food and the drink given to others, he will find no rest either by day or by night.

250. He in whom that feeling is destroyed, and taken out with the very root, finds rest by day and by night.

251. There is no fire like passion, there is no shark like hatred, there is no snare like folly, there is no torrent like greed.

252. The fault of others is easily perceived, but that of oneself is difficult to perceive; a man winnows his neighbour's faults like chaff, but his own fault he hides, as a cheat hides the bad die from the player.

253. If a man looks after the faults of others, and is always inclined to be offended, his own passions will grow, and he is far from the destruction of passions.

254. There is no path through the air, a man is not a Samana outwardly. The world delights in vanity, the Tathâgatas (the Buddhas) are free from vanity.

255. There is no path through the air, a man is not a Samana outwardly. No creatures are eternal; but the awakened (Buddha) are never shaken.

235. Uyyoga seems to mean departure. See Buddhaghosa's commentary on verse 152, p. 319, l. 1; Fausböll, Five Gâtakas, p. 35.

236. 'An island,' for a drowning man to save himself; (see verse 25.) It is well known that Dîpankara is the name of one of the former Buddhas, and it is also used as an appellative of the Buddha, but this name is derived from dîpo, 'a lamp,' and has nothing to do with dîpa, used metaphorically here and elsewhere in the sense of resting-place, shelter, or even Nirvâna; see Childers, s.v. dîpo.

239. This verse is the foundation of the thirty-fourth section of the Sûtra of the forty-two sections; see Beal, Catena, p. 201; Suttanipâta, v. 962.

241. On atidhonakârin, see Morris, J. P. T. S. 1887, p. 100.

244. Pakkhandin is identified by Dr. Fausböll with praskandin, one who jumps forward, insults, or, as Buddhaghosa explains it, one who meddles with other people's business, an interloper. At all events, it is a term of reproach, and, as it would seem, of theological reproach.

246. On the five principal commandments which are recapitulated in verses 246 and 247, see Buddhaghosha's Parables, p. 153.

248. Cf. Mahâbhârata XII, 4055, yeshâm vrittis ka samyatâ. See also verse 307.

249. This verse has evidently regard to the feelings of the Bhikshus or mendicants who receive either much or little, and who are exhorted not to be envious if others receive more than they themselves. Several of the Parables illustrate this feeling.

251. Dr. Fausböll translates gaho by 'captivitas,' Dr. Weber by 'fetter.' I take it in the same sense as grâha in Manu VI, 78; and Buddhaghosa does the same, though he assigns to grâha a more general meaning, viz. anything that seizes, whether an evil spirit (yakkha), a serpent (agagara), or a crocodile (kumbhîla).

Greed or thirst is represented as a river in Lalita-vistara, ed. Calc. p. 482, trishnâ-nadî tivegâ prasoshitâ me gñânasûryena, 'the wild river of thirst is dried up by the sun of my knowledge.'

252. See Childers, Notes, p. 7; St. Matthew vii. 3.

253. As to âsava, 'appetite, passion,' see note to verse 39.

254. I have translated this verse very freely, and not in accordance with Buddhaghosa's commentary. Dr. Fausböll proposed to translate, 'No one who is outside the Buddhist community can walk through the air, but only a Samana;' and the same view is taken by Professor Weber, though he arrives at it by a different construction. Now it is perfectly true that the idea of magical powers (riddhi) which enable saints to walk through the air, &c., occurs in the Dhammapada, see v. 175, note. But the Dhammapada may contain earlier and later verses, and in that case our verse might be an early protest on the part of Buddha against

the belief in such miraculous powers. We know how Buddha himself protested against his disciples being called upon to perform vulgar miracles. 'I command my disciples not to work miracles,' he said, 'but to hide their good deeds, and to show their sins' (Burnouf, Introd. p. 170). It would be in harmony with this sentiment if we translated our verse as I have done. As to bahira, I should take it in the sense of 'external,' as opposed to adhyâtmika, or 'internal;' and the meaning would be, 'a Samana is not a Samana by outward acts, but by his heart.' D'Alwis translates (p. 85): 'There is no footprint in the air; there is not a Samana out of the pale of the Buddhist community.'

Prapañka, which I have here translated by 'vanity,' seems to include the whole host of human weaknesses; cf. v. 196, where it is explained by tamhâditthimânapapañka; in our verse by tamhâdisu papañkesu: cf. Lalita-vistara, p. 564, anâlayam nishprapañkam anutpâdam asambhavam (dharmakakram). As to Tathâgata, a name of Buddha, cf. Burnouf, Introd. p. 75.

255. Sankhâra for samskâra; cf. note to verse 203. Creature does not, as Mr. D'Alwis (p. 69) supposes, involve the Christian conception of creation. Buddhaghosa takes sankhârâ as the five skandhas.

19

The Just

256, 257. A man is not just if he carries a matter by violence; no, he who distinguishes both right and wrong, who is learned and guides others, not by violence, but by the same law, being a guardian of the law and intelligent, he is called just.

258. A man is not learned because he talks much; he who is patient, free from hatred and fear, he is called learned.

259. A man is not a supporter of the law because he talks much; even if a man has learnt little, but sees the law bodily, he is a supporter of the law, a man who never neglects the law.

260. A man is not an elder because his head is grey; his age may be ripe, but he is called 'Old-in-vain.'

261. He in whom there is truth, virtue, pity, restraint, moder-

ation, he who is free from impurity and is wise, he is called an elder.

262. An envious, stingy, dishonest man does not become respectable by means of much talking only, or by the beauty of his complexion.

263. He in whom all this is destroyed, and taken out with the very root, he, when freed from hatred and wise, is called respectable.

264. Not by tonsure does an undisciplined man who speaks falsehood become a Samana; can a man be a Samana who is still held captive by desire and greediness?

265. He who always quiets the evil, whether small or large, he is called a Samana (a quiet man), because he has quieted all evil.

266. A man is not a mendicant (Bhikshu) simply because he asks others for alms; he who adopts the whole law is a Bhikshu, not he who only begs.

267. He who is above good and evil, who is chaste, who with care passes through the world, he indeed is called a Bhikshu.

268, 269. A man is not a Muni because he observes silence (mona, i.e. mauna), if he is foolish and ignorant; but the wise who, as with the balance, chooses the good and avoids evil, he is a Muni, and is a Muni thereby; he who in this world weighs both sides is called a Muni.

270. A man is not an elect (Ariya) because he injures living creatures; because he has pity on all living creatures, therefore is a man
called Ariya.

271, 272. Not only by discipline and vows, not only by much
learning, not by entering into a trance, not by sleeping alone, do
I earn the happiness of release which no worldling can know.
O Bhikshu, he who has obtained the extinction of desires, has
obtained confidence.

---

259. Buddhaghosa here takes law (dhamma) in the sense of the four great
truths, see note to verse 190. Could dhammam kâyena passati mean, 'he observes
the law in his acts, or sees the law with his bodily eyes'? Hardly, if we compare
expressions like dhammam vipassato, v. 373.

265. This is a curious etymology, because it shows that at the time when
this verse was written, the original meaning of sramana had been forgotten. Sramana meant originally, in the language of the Brahmans, a man who performed
hard penances, from sram, 'to work hard,' &c. When it became the name of the
Buddhist ascetics, the language had changed, and sramana was pronounced samana. Now there is another Sanskrit root, sam, 'to quiet,' which in Pâli becomes
likewise sam, and from this root sam, 'to quiet,' and not from sram, 'to tire,' did
the popular etymology of the day and the writer of our verse derive the title of
the Buddhist priests. The original form sramana became known to the Greeks
as Σαρμᾶναι, that of samana as Σαμαναῖοι; the former through Megasthenes, the
latter through Bardesanes, 80–60 B.C. (See Lassen, Indische Alterthumskunde,
II, 700.) The Chinese Shamen and the Tungusian Shamen do not come from
the same source, though this has sometimes been doubted. See Schott, Über die
doppelte Bedeutung des Wortes Schamane, in the Philosophical Transactions of
the Berlin Academy, 1842, p. 463 seq.

266–270. The etymologies here given of the ordinary titles of the followers
of Buddha are entirely fanciful, and are curious only as showing how the people who spoke Pâli had lost the etymological consciousness of their language.
A Bhikshu is a beggar, i.e. a Buddhist friar who has left his family and lives
entirely on alms. Muni is a sage, hence Sâkya-muni, a name of Gautama. Muni
comes from man, 'to think,' and from muni comes mauna, 'silence.' Ariya, again,
is the general name of those who embrace a religious life. It meant originally

'respectable, noble.' In verse 270 it seems as if the writer wished to guard against deriving ariya from ari, 'enemy.' See note to verse 22.

272. See Childers, Notes, p. 7. Nekkhamana-sukham is explained by the commentator as anâgami-sukham, the happiness of one who can be born again once only in the world of Brahma. The same commentator takes Bhikkhu as a vocative. The last line is obscure, and Fausböll with his usual modesty adds, num recte alterum hemistichium intellexerim docti videant. The text of the commentary is so imperfect that in its present state it cannot help us much. Following its indications, however, Childers proposed an emendation, Bhikkhu vissâsam mâ âpâdi, lit. priest, enter not into confidence. Bhikkhu may, of course, be vocative or nominative. I formerly followed Fausböll's conjecture, but I should now prefer to take Bhikkhu as a nominative, referring it to the person who is speaking, i.e. I or the Bhikshu in general, has obtained confidence or peace of mind, as soon as he has obtained the extinction of passions. Âpâdi is here not a first, but a third person. Kuhn, Pâli Grammatik, p. 109. Appatto stands for âpatto, Sk. âpanno. See Kuhn, Pâli Grammatik, p. 119. Athavâ, in v. 270, means or, and corresponds to vâ; it can mean nothing else here but what it means everywhere, whether in Sanskrit or in Pâli.

20

The Way

273. The best of ways is the eightfold; the best of truths the four words; the best of virtues passionlessness; the best of men he who has eyes to see.

274. This is the way, there is no other that leads to the purifying of intelligence. Go on this path! This is the confusion of Mâra (the tempter).

275. If you go on this way, you will make an end of pain! The way was preached by me, when I had understood the removal of the thorns (in the flesh).

276. You yourself must make an effort. The Tathâgatas (Buddhas) are only preachers. The thoughtful who enter the way are freed from the bondage of Mâra.

277. 'All created things perish,' he who knows and sees this becomes passive in pain; this is the way to purity.

278. 'All created things are grief and pain,' he who knows and sees
this becomes passive in pain; this is the way that leads to purity.

279. 'All forms are unreal,' he who knows and sees this becomes
passive in pain; this is the way that leads to purity.

280. He who does not rouse himself when it is time to rise, who,
though young and strong, is full of sloth, whose will and thought
are weak, that lazy and idle man never finds the way to knowledge.

281. Watching his speech, well restrained in mind, let a man never
commit any wrong with his body! Let a man but keep these three
roads of action clear, and he will achieve the way which is taught
by the wise.

282. Through zeal knowledge is gotten, through lack of zeal
knowledge is lost; let a man who knows this double path of gain
and loss thus place himself that knowledge may grow.

283. Cut down the whole forest (of desires), not a tree only! Danger comes out of the forest (of desires). When you have cut down
both the forest (of desires) and its undergrowth, then, Bhikshus,
you will be rid of the forest and of desires!

284. So long as the desire of man towards women, even the

smallest, is not destroyed, so long is his mind in bondage, as the calf that drinks milk is to its mother.

285. Cut out the love of self, like an autumn lotus, with thy hand! Cherish the road of peace. Nirvâna has been shown by Sugata (Buddha).

286. 'Here I shall dwell in the rain, here in winter and summer,' thus the fool meditates, and does not think of death.

287. Death comes and carries off that man, honoured for his children and flocks, his mind distracted, as a flood carries off a sleeping village.

288. Sons are no help, nor a father, nor relations; there is no help from kinsfolk for one whom death has seized.
289. A wise and well-behaved man who knows the meaning of this, should quickly clear the way that leads to Nirvâna.

---

273. The eightfold or eight-membered way is the technical term for the way by which Nirvâna is attained. (See Burnouf, Lotus, p. 519.) This very way constitutes the fourth of the Four Truths, or the four words of truth, viz. Duhkha, 'pain;' Samudaya, 'origin;' Nirodha, 'destruction;' Mârga, 'road.' (Lotus, p. 517.) See note to verse 178. For another explanation of the Mârga, or 'way,' see Hardy, Eastern Monachism, p. 280.

274. The last line means, 'this following the true path is to confound Mâra,' i.e. the discomfiture of Mâra.

275. The salyas, 'arrows or thorns,' are the sokasalya, 'the arrows of grief.' Buddha himself is called mahâsalya-hartâ, 'the great remover of thorns.' (Lalitavistara, p. 550; Mahâbh. XII, 5616.)

277. See v. 255. Nibbeda is sthâyibhâva.

278. See v. 203.

279. Dhamma stands evidently for saṅkhâra, and means the five khandha, i.e. what constitutes a living body.

281. Cf. Beal, Catena, p. 159.

282. Bhûri was rightly translated 'intelligentia' by Dr. Fausböll. Dr. Weber renders it by 'Gedeihen,' but the commentator distinctly explains it as 'vast knowledge,' and in the technical sense the word occurs after vidyâ and before medhâ, in the Lalita-vistara, p. 541.

283. A pun, vana meaning both 'lust' and 'forest.' See some mistaken remarks on this verse in D'Alwis, Nirvâna, p. 86, and some good remarks in Childers, Notes, p. 7.

285. Cf. Gâtaka, vol. i, p. 183.

286. Antarâya, according to the commentator, ĝivitântarâya, means interitus, death, it does not mean here an obstacle only.

287. See notes to verse 47, Thiessen, Kisâgotamî, p. 11, and Mahâbh. XII, 9944, 6540. To clear is used in the sense of making clear or easy to enter, like our own to clear the way.

21

Miscellaneous

290. If by leaving a small pleasure one sees a great pleasure, let a wise man leave the small pleasure, and look to the great.

291. He who, by causing pain to others, wishes to obtain pleasure for himself, he, entangled in the bonds of hatred, will never be free from hatred.

292. What ought to be done is neglected, what ought not to be done is done; the desires of unruly, thoughtless people are always increasing.

293. But they whose whole watchfulness is always directed to their body, who do not follow what ought not to be done, and who steadfastly do what ought to be done, the desires of such watchful and wise people will come to an end.

294. A true Brâhmana goes scatheless, though he have killed father and mother, and two valiant kings, though he has destroyed a kingdom with all its subjects.

295. A true Brâhmana goes scatheless, though he have killed father and mother, and two holy kings, and an eminent man besides.

296. The disciples of Gotama (Buddha) are always well awake, and their thoughts day and night are always set on Buddha.

297. The disciples of Gotama are always well awake, and their thoughts day and night are always set on the law.

298. The disciples of Gotama are always well awake, and their thoughts day and night are always set on the church.

299. The disciples of Gotama are always well awake, and their thoughts day and night are always set on their body.

300. The disciples of Gotama are always well awake, and their mind day and night always delights in compassion.

301. The disciples of Gotama are always well awake, and their mind day and night always delights in meditation.

302. It is hard to leave the world (to become a friar), it is hard to enjoy the world; hard is the monastery, painful are the houses; painful it is to dwell with equals (to share everything in common), and

the itinerant mendicant is beset with pain. Therefore let no man be an itinerant mendicant, and he will not be beset with pain.

303. A man full of faith, if endowed with virtue and glory, is respected, whatever place he may choose.

304. Good people shine from afar, like the snowy mountains; bad people are not seen, like arrows shot by night.

305. Sitting alone, lying down alone, walking alone without ceasing, and alone subduing himself, let a man be happy near the edge of a forest.

---

292. Cf. Beal, Catena, p. 264.

294, 295. These two verses are either meant to show that a truly holy man who, by accident, commits all these crimes is guiltless, or they refer to some particular event in Buddha's history. The commentator is so startled that he explains them allegorically. Mr. D'Alwis is very indignant that I should have supposed Buddha capable of pardoning parricide. 'Can it be believed,' he writes, 'that a Teacher, who held life, even the life of the minutest insect, nay, even a living tree, in such high estimation as to prevent its wanton destruction, has declared that the murder of a Brâhma*n*a, to whom he accorded reverence, along with his own Sangha, was blameless?' D'Alwis, Nirvâ*n*a, p. 88. Though something might be said in reply, considering the antecedents of king Agâta*s*atru, the patron of Buddha, and stories such as that quoted by the commentator on the Dhammapada (Beal, l.c. p. 150), or in Der Weise und der Thor, p. 306, still these two verses are startling, and I am not aware that Buddha has himself drawn the conclusion, which has been drawn by others, viz. that those who have reached the highest Sambodhi, and are in fact no longer themselves, are outside the domain of good and bad, and beyond the reach of guilt. Verses like 39 and 412 admit of a different explanation. Still our verses being miscellaneous extracts, might possibly have been taken from a work in which such an opinion was advanced, and I find that Mr. Childers, no mean admirer of Buddha, was not shocked by my explanation. 'In my judgment,' he says, 'this verse is intended to express in a forcible manner the Buddhist doctrine that the Arhat cannot commit a serious sin,' 'na hanti, na *k*a hanyate.' However, we have met before with far-fetched puns in these verses, and it is not impossible that the native commentators were right after all in seeing some puns or riddles in this verse. D'Alwis, following the commentary, explains mother as lust, father as pride, the two valiant kings as heretical systems, and the realm as sensual pleasure, while veyyaggha is taken by him for a place infested with the tigers of obstruction against final beatitude. Some confirmation of this interpretation is supplied by a passage in the third book of the Laṅkâvatâra-sûtra, as quoted by Mr. Beal in his translation of the Dhammapada, Introduction, p. 5. Here a stanza is quoted as having been recited by Buddha, in explanation of a similar startling utterance which he had made to Mahâmati:

> 'Lust, or carnal desire, this is the Mother,
> Ignorance, this is the Father,
> The highest point of knowledge, this is Buddha,
> All the klesas, these are the Rahats,
> The five skandhas, these are the Priests;
> To commit the five unpardonable sins
> Is to destroy these five
> And yet not suffer the pains of hell.'

The Laṅkâvatâra-sûtra was translated into Chinese by Bodhiruki (508–511); when it was written is doubtful. See also Gâtaka, vol. ii, p. 263.

302. This verse is difficult, and I give my translation as tentative only. Childers (Notes, p. 11) has removed some, not all difficulties, and I have been chiefly guided by the interpretation put on the verse by the Chinese translator; see Beal, Dhammapada, p. 137.

305. Vanânte, within the forest, according to a pun pointed out before (v. 283), means both 'at the end of a forest,' and 'at the end of desires.'

22

The Downward Course

306. He who says what is not, goes to hell; he also who, having done a thing, says I have not done it. After death both are equal, they are men with evil deeds in the next world.

307. Many men whose shoulders are covered with the yellow gown are ill-conditioned and unrestrained; such evil-doers by their evil deeds go to hell.

308. Better it would be to swallow a heated iron ball, like flaring fire, than that a bad unrestrained fellow should live on the charity of the land.

309. Four things does a reckless man gain who covets his neighbour's wife,—demerit, an uncomfortable bed, thirdly, punishment, and lastly, hell.

310. There is demerit, and the evil way (to hell), there is the short pleasure of the frightened in the arms of the frightened, and the king imposes heavy punishment; therefore let no man think of his neighbour's wife.

311. As a grass-blade, if badly grasped, cuts the arm, badly-practised asceticism leads to hell.

312. An act carelessly performed, a broken vow, and hesitating obedience to discipline (Brahma*k*ariyam), all this brings no great reward.

313. If anything is to be done, let a man do it, let him attack it vigorously! A careless pilgrim only scatters the dust of his passions more widely.

314. An evil deed is better left undone, for a man repents of it afterwards; a good deed is better done, for having done it, one does not repent.

315. Like a well-guarded frontier fort, with defences within and without, so let a man guard himself. Not a moment should escape, for they who allow the right moment to pass, suffer pain when they are in hell.

316. They who are ashamed of what they ought not to be ashamed of, and are not ashamed of what they ought to be ashamed of, such men, embracing false doctrines, enter the evil path.

317. They who fear when they ought not to fear, and fear not when they ought to fear, such men, embracing false doctrines, enter the evil path.

318. They who see sin where there is no sin, and see no sin where there is sin, such men, embracing false doctrines, enter the evil path.

319. They who see sin where there is sin, and no sin where there is no sin, such men, embracing the true doctrine, enter the good path.

---

306. I translate niraya, 'the exit, the downward course, the evil path,' by 'hell,' because the meaning assigned to that ancient mythological name by Christian writers comes so near to the Buddhist idea of niraya, that it is difficult not to believe in some actual contact between these two streams of thought. See also Mahâbh. XII, 7176. Cf. Gâtaka, vol. ii, p. 416; Suttanipâta, v. 660.

307, 308. These two verses are said to be taken from the Vinayapitaka I, 4, 1; D'Alwis, Nirvâna, p. 29.

308. The charity of the land, i.e. the alms given, from a sense of religious duty, to every mendicant that asks for it.

309, 310. The four things mentioned in verse 309 seem to be repeated in verse 310. Therefore, apuññalâbha, 'demerit,' is the same in both: gatî pâpikâ must be niraya; danda corresponds to nindâ, and ratî thokikâ explains the anikâmaseyyam. Buddhaghosa takes the same view of the meaning of anikâmaseyya, i.e. yathâ ikkhati evam seyyam alabhitvâ, antikkhitam parittakam eva kâlam seyyam labhati, 'not obtaining the rest as he wishes it, he obtains it, as he does not wish it, for a short time only.'

313. As to raga meaning 'dust' and 'passion,' see Buddhaghosha's Parables, pp. 65, 66.

23

The Elephant

320. Silently I endured abuse as the elephant in battle endures the arrow sent from the bow: for the world is ill-natured.

321. They lead a tamed elephant to battle, the king mounts a tamed elephant; the tamed is the best among men, he who silently endures abuse.

322. Mules are good, if tamed, and noble Sindhu horses, and elephants with large tusks; but he who tames himself is better still.

323. For with these animals does no man reach the untrodden country (Nirvâna), where a tamed man goes on a tamed animal, viz. on his own well-tamed self.

324. The elephant called Dhanapâlaka, his temples running with

pungent sap, and who is difficult to hold, does not eat a morsel when bound; the elephant longs for the elephant grove.

325. If a man becomes fat and a great eater, if he is sleepy and rolls himself about, that fool, like a hog fed on grains, is born again and again.

326. This mind of mine went formerly wandering about as it liked, as it listed, as it pleased; but I shall now hold it in thoroughly, as the rider who holds the hook holds in the furious elephant.

327. Be not thoughtless, watch your thoughts! Draw yourself out of the evil way, like an elephant sunk in mud.

328. If a man find a prudent companion who walks with him, is wise, and lives soberly, he may walk with him, overcoming all dangers, happy, but considerate.

329. If a man find no prudent companion who walks with him, is wise, and lives soberly, let him walk alone, like a king who has left his conquered country behind,—like an elephant in the forest.

330. It is better to live alone, there is no companionship with a fool; let a man walk alone, let him commit no sin, with few wishes, like an elephant in the forest.

331. If the occasion arises, friends are pleasant; enjoyment is pleasant, whatever be the cause; a good work is pleasant in the hour of death; the giving up of all grief is pleasant.

332. Pleasant in the world is the state of a mother, pleasant the state of a father, pleasant the state of a Samana, pleasant the state of a Brâhmana.

333. Pleasant is virtue lasting to old age, pleasant is a faith firmly rooted; pleasant is attainment of intelligence, pleasant is avoiding of sins.

---

320. The elephant is with the Buddhists the emblem of endurance and self-restraint. Thus Buddha himself is called Nâga, 'the Elephant' (Lal.Vist. p. 553), or Mahânâga, 'the great Elephant' (Lal.Vist. p. 553), and in one passage (Lal.Vist. p. 554) the reason of this name is given, by stating that Buddha was sudânta, 'well-tamed,' like an elephant. He descended from heaven in the form of an elephant to be born on earth. On titikkhisam, see Childers, s.v. titikkhati.

See also Manu VI, 47, ativâdâms titiksheta.

323. I read, as suggested by Dr. Fausböll, yath' attanâ sudantena danto dantena gakkhati (cf. verse 160). The India Office MS. reads na hi etehi thânehi gakkheya agatam disam, yath' attânam sudantena danto dantena gakkhati. As to thânehi instead of yânehi, see verse 224.

325. On nivâpa, see B.-R. Petersburg Dict. s.v.

326. Yoniso, i e. yonisah, is rendered by Dr. Fausböll 'sapientiâ,' and this is the meaning ascribed to yoni by many Buddhist authorities. But the reference to Hemakandra (ed. Boehtlingk and Rieu, p. 281) shows clearly that it meant 'origin,' or 'cause.' Yoniso occurs frequently as a mere adverb, meaning 'thoroughly, radically' (Dhammapada, p. 359), and yoniso manasikâra (Dhammapada, p. 110) means 'taking to heart' or 'minding thoroughly,' or, what is nearly the same, 'wisely.' In the Lalita-vistara, p. 41, the commentator has clearly mistaken yonisah, changing it to ye x niso, and explaining it by yamanisam, whereas M. Foucaux has rightly translated it by 'depuis l'origine.' Professor Weber suspected in yonisah a double entendre, but even grammar would show that our author is innocent of it. In Lalita-vistara, p. 544, l. 4, ayonisa occurs in the sense of error.

327. Appamâdarata, not delighting in pamâda.

328, 329. Cf. Suttanipâta, vv. 44, 45.

332. The commentator throughout takes these words, like matteyyatâ, &c., to signify, not the status of a mother, or maternity, but reverence shown to a mother.

24

Thirst

334. The thirst of a thoughtless man grows like a creeper; he runs from life to life, like a monkey seeking fruit in the forest.

335. Whomsoever this fierce poisonous thirst overcomes, in this world, his sufferings increase like the abounding Bîra*n*a grass.

336. But from him who overcomes this fierce thirst, difficult to be conquered in this world, sufferings fall off, like water-drops from a lotus leaf.

337. This salutary word I tell you, 'Do ye, as many as are here assembled, dig up the root of thirst, as he who wants the sweet-scented Usîra root must dig up the Bîra*n*a grass, that Mâra (the tempter) may not crush you again and again, as the stream crushes the reeds.'

338. As a tree, even though it has been cut down, is firm so long as its root is safe, and grows again, thus, unless the feeders of thirst are destroyed, this pain (of life) will return again and again.

339. He whose thirty-six streams are strongly flowing in the channels of pleasure, the waves will carry away that misguided man, viz. his desires which are set on passion.

340. The channels run everywhere, the creeper (of passion) stands sprouting; if you see the creeper springing up, cut its root by means of knowledge.

341. A creature's pleasures are extravagant and luxurious; given up to pleasure and deriving happiness, men undergo (again and again) birth and decay.

342. Beset with lust, men run about like a snared hare; held in fetters and bonds, they undergo pain for a long time, again and again.

343. Beset with lust, men run about like a snared hare; let therefore the mendicant drive out thirst, by striving after passionlessness for himself.

344. He who having got rid of the forest (of lust) (i.e. after having reached Nirvâna) gives himself over to forest-life (i.e. to lust), and who, when free from the forest (i.e. from lust), runs to the forest (i.e. to lust), look at that man! though free, he runs into bondage.

345. Wise people do not call that a strong fetter which is made of

iron, wood, or hemp; passionately strong is the care for precious stones and rings, for sons and a wife.

346. That fetter wise people call strong which drags down, yields, but is difficult to undo; after having cut this at last, people leave the world, free from cares, and leaving the pleasures of love behind.

347. Those who are slaves to passions, run down the stream (of desires), as a spider runs down the web which he has made himself; when they have cut this, at last, wise people go onwards, free from cares, leaving all pain behind.

348. Give up what is before, give up what is behind, give up what is between, when thou goest to the other shore of existence; if thy mind is altogether free, thou wilt not again enter into birth and decay.

349. If a man is tossed about by doubts, full of strong passions, and yearning only for what is delightful, his thirst will grow more and more, and he will indeed make his fetters strong.

350. If a man delights in quieting doubts, and, always reflecting, dwells on what is not delightful (the impurity of the body, &c.), he certainly will remove, nay, he will cut the fetter of Mâra.

351. He who has reached the consummation, who does not tremble, who is without thirst and without sin, he has broken all the thorns of life: this will be his last body.

352. He who is without thirst and without affection, who understands the words and their interpretation, who knows the order of letters (those which are before and which are after), he has received his last body, he is called the great sage, the great man.

353. 'I have conquered all, I know all, in all conditions of life I am free from taint; I have left all, and through the destruction of thirst I am free; having learnt myself, whom should I indicate (as my teacher)?'

354. The gift of the law exceeds all gifts; the sweetness of the law exceeds all sweetness; the delight in the law exceeds all delights; the extinction of thirst overcomes all pain.

355. Riches destroy the foolish, if they look not for the other shore; the foolish by his thirst for riches destroys himself, as if he were (destroying) others.

356. The fields are damaged by weeds, mankind is damaged by passion: therefore a gift bestowed on the passionless brings great reward.

357. The fields are damaged by weeds, mankind is damaged by hatred: therefore a gift bestowed on those who do not hate brings great reward.

358. The fields are damaged by weeds, mankind is damaged by vanity: therefore a gift bestowed on those who are free from vanity brings great reward.

359. The fields are damaged by weeds, mankind is damaged by lust: therefore a gift bestowed on those who are free from lust brings great reward.

---

334. This is explained by a story in the Chinese translation. Beal, Dhammapada, p. 148.

335. Bîra*na* grass is the Andropogon muricatum, and the scented root of it is called U*s*îra (cf. verse 337).

338. On Anusaya, i.e. Anu*s*aya (Anlage), see Wassiljew, Der Buddhismus, p. 240 seq.

339. The thirty-six channels, which are divided by the commentator into eighteen external and eighteen internal, are explained by Burnouf (Lotus, p. 649), from a gloss of the Ginaala*n*kâra: 'L'indication précise des affections dont un Buddha acte indépendant, affections qui sont au nombre de dix-huit, nous est fourni par la glose d'un livre appartenant aux Buddhistes de Ceylan,' &c. Gray, however, takes them as the six organs of sense, the six objects of sense, in relation (1) to a desire for sensual pleasure, (2) to a desire for existence, and (3) to a desire for non-existence. Subhûti gives the right reading as manâpassavanâ; cf. Childers, Notes, p. 12.

Vâhâ, which Dr. Fausböll translates by 'equi,' should be vahâ, 'undae.' Cf. Suttanipâta, v. 1034.

344. This verse seems again full of puns, all connected with the twofold meaning of vana, 'forest and lust.' By replacing 'forest' by 'lust,' we may translate: 'He who, when free from lust, gives himself up to lust, who, when removed from lust runs into lust, look at that man,' &c. Nibbana, though with a short a, may be intended to remind the hearer of Nibbâna. The right reading, according to Childers, Notes, p. 8, is nibbanatho.

345. Apekhâ, apekshâ, 'care;' see Manu VI, 41, 49; Suttanipâta, v. 37; and Gâtaka, vol. ii, p. 140.

346. Paribbag, i.e. parivrag; see Manu VI, 41.

347. The commentator explains the simile of the spider as follows: 'As a spider, after having made its thread-web, sits in the middle, and after killing with a violent rush a butterfly or a fly which has fallen in its circle, drinks its juice, returns, and sits again in the same place, in the same manner creatures who are given to passions, depraved by hatred, and maddened by wrath, run along the stream of thirst which they have made themselves, and cannot cross it,' &c.

352. As to nirutti, and its technical meaning among the Buddhists, see Burnouf, Lotus, p. 841. Fausböll translates 'niruttis vocabulorum peritus,' which may be right, if we take nirutti in the sense of the language of the Scriptures. See

note to verse 363. Could not sannipâta mean samhitâ or sannikarsha? Sannipâta occurs in the Sâkala-prâtisâkhya, but with a different meaning.

353. Cf. Suttanipâta, v. 210. The commentator explains that this verse was spoken by Buddha on his way to Bârânasî, in answer to Upaka, who had asked him who his teacher was, when Buddha asserted that he had no teacher. Childers accepts this explanation, s.v. uddigati. See also Lalita-vistara XXVI, ed. Calc. p. 526 seq., and read tenopaka gino hy aham.

354. The dhammadâna, or 'gift of the law,' is the technical term for instruction in the Buddhist religion. See Buddhaghosha's Parables, p. 160, where the story of the Sakkadevarâga is told, and where a free rendering of our verse is given.

358. 'Vanity and vexation of spirit,' Ecclesiastes.

25

The Bhikshu (Mendicant)

360. Restraint in the eye is good, good is restraint in the ear, in the nose restraint is good, good is restraint in the tongue.

361. In the body restraint is good, good is restraint in speech, in thought restraint is good, good is restraint in all things. A Bhikshu, restrained in all things, is freed from all pain.

362. He who controls his hand, he who controls his feet, he who controls his speech, he who is well controlled, he who delights inwardly, who is collected, who is solitary and content, him they call Bhikshu.

363. The Bhikshu who controls his mouth, who speaks wisely and calmly, who teaches the meaning and the law, his word is sweet.

364. He who dwells in the law, delights in the law, meditates on

the law, recollects the law, that Bhikshu will never fall away from
the true law.

365. Let him not despise what he has received, nor ever envy others: a mendicant who envies others does not obtain peace of mind.

366. A Bhikshu who, though he receives little, does not despise
what he has received, even the gods will praise him, if his life is
pure, and if he is not slothful.

367. He who never identifies himself with name and form, and
does not grieve over what is no more, he indeed is called a Bhikshu.

368. The Bhikshu who behaves with kindness, who is happy in
the doctrine of Buddha, will reach the quiet place (Nirvâna),
happiness arising from the cessation of natural inclinations.

369. O Bhikshu, empty this boat! if emptied, it will go quickly;
having cut off passion and hatred, thou wilt go to Nirvâna.

370. Cut off the five (fetters), leave the five, rise above the five.
A Bhikshu, who has escaped from the five fetters, he is called
Oghatinna, 'saved from the flood.'

371. Meditate, O Bhikshu, and be not heedless! Do not direct
thy thought to what gives pleasure, that thou mayest not for thy
heedlessness have to swallow the iron ball (in hell), and that thou
mayest not cry out when burning, 'This is pain.'

372. Without knowledge there is no meditation, without

meditation there is no knowledge: he who has knowledge and meditation is near unto Nirvâna.

373. A Bhikshu who has entered his empty house, and whose mind is tranquil, feels a more than human delight when he sees the law clearly.

374. As soon as he has considered the origin and destruction of the elements (khandha) of the body, he finds happiness and joy which belong to those who know the immortal (Nirvâna).

375. And this is the beginning here for a wise Bhikshu: watchfulness over the senses, contentedness, restraint under the law; keep noble friends whose life is pure, and who are not slothful.

376. Let him live in charity, let him be perfect in his duties; then in the fulness of delight he will make an end of suffering.

377. As the Vassikâ plant sheds its withered flowers, men should shed passion and hatred, O ye Bhikshus!

378. The Bhikshu whose body and tongue and mind are quieted, who is collected, and has rejected the baits of the world, he is called quiet.

379. Rouse thyself by thyself, examine thyself by thyself, thus self-protected and attentive wilt thou live happily, O Bhikshu!

380. For self is the lord of self, self is the refuge of self; therefore curb thyself as the merchant curbs a noble horse.

381. The Bhikshu, full of delight, who is happy in the doctrine of Buddha will reach the quiet place (Nirvâna), happiness consisting in the cessation of natural inclinations.

382. He who, even as a young Bhikshu, applies himself to the doctrine of Buddha, brightens up this world, like the moon when free from clouds.

---

363. On artha and dharma, see Stanislas Julien, Les Avadânas, I, 217, note: 'Les quatre connaissances sont; 1° la connaissance du sens (artha); 2° la connaissance de la Loi (dharma); 3° la connaissance des explications (niroukti); 4° la connaissance de l'intelligence (prâtibhâna).'

364. The expression dhammârâmo, 'having his garden or delight (Lustgarten) in the law,' is well matched by the Brahmanic expression ekârâma, i.e. nirdvandva (Mahâbh. XIII, 1930). Cf. Suttanipâta, v. 326; Dhammapada, v. 32.

367. Nâmarûpa is here used again in its technical sense of mind and body, neither of which, however, is with the Buddhists âtman, or 'self.' Asat, 'what is not,' may therefore mean the same as nâmarûpa, or we may take it in the sense of what is no more, as, for instance, the beauty or youth of the body, the vigour of the mind, &c.

368. See Childers, Notes, p. 11, who translates, 'where existence is no more:' but if we take saṅkhâra in the plural, it may mean states of the mind, or predispositions, inclinations, good, bad, or indifferent. Verse 383 supports Childers' version.

370. Morris, J. P. T. S. 1887, p. 116, takes uttaribhâvaye in the sense of to cultivate especially. Fausböll translates removeat. The five are differently explained by the commentator. See also Childers, s.v. saṃyogana.

371. The swallowing of hot iron balls is considered as a punishment in hell; see verse 308. Professor Weber has perceived the right meaning of bhavassu, which can only be bhâvayasva, but I doubt whether the rest of his rendering is right, for who would swallow an iron ball by accident?

372. Cf. Beal, Catena, p. 247.

375. Cf. Suttanipâta, v. 337.

381. See verse 368. D'Alwis translates, 'dissolution of the saṅkhâras (elements of existence).'

26

The Brâhmana (Arhat)

383. Stop the stream valiantly, drive away the desires, O Brâhmana! When you have understood the destruction of all that was made, you will understand that which was not made.

384. If the Brâhmana has reached the other shore in both laws (in restraint and contemplation), all bonds vanish from him who has obtained knowledge.

385. He for whom there is neither the hither nor the further shore, nor both, him, the fearless and unshackled, I call indeed a Brâhmana.

386. He who is thoughtful, blameless, settled, dutiful, without passions, and who has attained the highest end, him I call indeed a Brâhmana.

387. The sun is bright by day, the moon shines by night, the warrior is bright in his armour, the Brâhmana is bright in his meditation; but Buddha, the Awakened, is bright with splendour day and night.

388. Because a man is rid of evil, therefore he is called Brâhmana; because he walks quietly, therefore he is called Samana; because he has sent away his own impurities, therefore he is called Pravragita (Pabbagita, a pilgrim).

389. No one should attack a Brâhmana, but no Brâhmana (if attacked) should let himself fly at his aggressor! Woe to him who strikes a Brâhmana, more woe to him who flies at his aggressor!

390. It advantages a Brâhmana not a little if he holds his mind back from the pleasures of life; the more all wish to injure has vanished, the more all pain will cease.

391. Him I call indeed a Brâhmana who does not offend by body, word, or thought, and is controlled on these three points.

392. He from whom he may learn the law, as taught by the Well-awakened (Buddha), him let him worship assiduously, as the Brâhmana worships the sacrificial fire.

393. A man does not become a Brâhmana by his platted hair, by his family, or by birth; in whom there is truth and righteousness, he is blessed, he is a Brâhmana.

394. What is the use of platted hair, O fool! what of the raiment of goat-skins? Within thee there is ravening, but the outside thou makest clean.

395. The man who wears dirty raiments, who is emaciated and covered with veins, who meditates alone in the forest, him I call indeed a Brâhmana.

396. I do not call a man a Brâhmana because of his origin or of his mother. He is indeed arrogant, and he is wealthy: but the poor, who is free from all attachments, him I call indeed a Brâhmana.

397. Him I call indeed a Brâhmana who after cutting all fetters never trembles, is free from bonds and unshackled.

398. Him I call indeed a Brâhmana who after cutting the strap and the thong, the rope with all that pertains to it, has destroyed all obstacles, and is awakened.

399. Him I call indeed a Brâhmana who, though he has committed no offence, endures reproach, stripes, and bonds, who has endurance for his force, and strength for his army.

400. Him I call indeed a Brâhmana who is free from anger, dutiful, virtuous, without appetites, who is subdued, and has received his last body.

401. Him I call indeed a Brâhmana who does not cling to sensual pleasures, like water on a lotus leaf, like a mustard seed on the point of a needle.

402. Him I call indeed a Brâhmana who, even here, knows the end of his own suffering, has put down his burden, and is unshackled.

403. Him I call indeed a Brâhmana whose knowledge is deep, who possesses wisdom, who knows the right way and the wrong, and has attained the highest end.

404. Him I call indeed a Brâhmana who keeps aloof both from laymen and from mendicants, who frequents no houses, and has but few desires.

405. Him I call indeed a Brâhmana who without hurting any creatures, whether feeble or strong, does not kill nor cause slaughter.

406. Him I call indeed a Brâhmana who is tolerant with the intolerant, mild with the violent, and free from greed among the greedy.

407. Him I call indeed a Brâhmana from whom anger and hatred, pride and hypocrisy have dropt like a mustard seed from the point of a needle.

408. Him I call indeed a Brâhmana who utters true speech, instructive and free from harshness, so that he offend no one.

409. Him I call indeed a Brâhmana who takes nothing in the world that is not given him, be it long or short, small or large, good or bad.

410. Him I call indeed a Brâhmana who fosters no desires for this world or for the next, has no inclinations, and is unshackled.

411. Him I call indeed a Brâhmana who has no interests, and when he has understood (the truth), does not say How, how? and who has reached the depth of the Immortal.

412. Him I call indeed a Brâhmana who in this world has risen above both ties, good and evil, who is free from grief, from sin, and from impurity.

413. Him I call indeed a Brâhmana who is bright like the moon, pure, serene, undisturbed, and in whom all gaiety is extinct.

414. Him I call indeed a Brâhmana who has traversed this miry road, the impassable world, difficult to pass, and its vanity, who has gone through, and reached the other shore, is thoughtful, steadfast, free from doubts, free from attachment, and content.

415. Him I call indeed a Brâhmana who in this world, having abandoned all desires, travels about without a home, and in whom all concupiscence is extinct.

416. Him I call indeed a Brâhmana who, having abandoned all longings, travels about without a home, and in whom all covetousness is extinct.

417. Him I call indeed a Brâhmana who, after leaving all bondage to men, has risen above all bondage to the gods, and is free from all and every bondage.

418. Him I call indeed a Brâhma*n*a who has left what gives plea-sure and what gives pain, who is cold, and free from all germs (of renewed life), the hero who has conquered all the worlds.

419. Him I call indeed a Brâhma*n*a who knows the destruction and the return of beings everywhere, who is free from bondage, welfaring (Sugata), and awakened (Buddha).

420. Him I call indeed a Brâhma*n*a whose path the gods do not know, nor spirits (Gandharvas), nor men, whose passions are ex-tinct, and who is an Arhat (venerable).

421. Him I call indeed a Brâhma*n*a who calls nothing his own, whether it be before, behind, or between, who is poor, and free from the love of the world.

422. Him I call indeed a Brâhma*n*a, the manly, the noble, the hero, the great sage, the conqueror, the indifferent, the accom-plished, the awakened.

423. Him I call indeed a Brâhma*n*a who knows his former abodes, who sees heaven and hell, has reached the end of births, is perfect in knowledge, a sage, and whose perfections are all perfect.

---

385. The exact meaning of the two shores is not quite clear, and the com-mentator who takes them in the sense of internal and external organs of sense, can hardly be right. See verse 86.

388. These would-be etymologies are again interesting as showing the de-cline of the etymological consciousness of the spoken language of India at the time when such etymologies became possible. But in order to derive Brâhma*n*a from vâh, it must have been pronounced bâhma*n*o; vâh, 'to remove,' occurs

frequently in the Buddhistical Sanskrit. Cf. Lal. Vist. p. 551, l. 1; 553, l. 7. See note to verse 265.

390. I am afraid I have taken too much liberty with this verse. Dr. Fausböll translates, 'Non Brâhma*n*ae hoc paulo melius, quando retentio fit mentis a jucundis.'

392. I have followed Childers, s.v. yo, in the translation of this verse.

393. Fausböll proposes to read ga*kk*â (gâtyâ). 'Both' in the first edition of my translation was a misprint for 'birth.'

394. I have not copied the language of the Bible more than I was justified in. The words are abbhantaran te gahana*m*, bâhira*m* parima*gg*asi, 'interna est abyssus, externum mundas.' Cf. Gâtaka, vol. i, p. 481.

395. The expression Kisan dhamanisanthatam is the Sanskrit k*ri*sa*m* dhamanîsantatam, the frequent occurrence of which in the Mahâbhârata has been pointed out by Boehtlingk, s.v. dhamani. It looks more like a Brâhmanic than like a Buddhist phrase.

396. From verse 396 to the first half of verse 423, the text of the Dhammapada agrees with the text of the Vasish*th*a-Bharadvâgasûtra. These verses are translated by D'Alwis in his Nirvâ*n*a, pp. 113–118, and again by Fausböll, Suttanipâta, v. 620 seq.

The text contains puns on ki*ñk*ana, which means 'wealth,' but also 'attachment;' cf. Childers, s.v.

398. D'Alwis points out a double entendre in these words. Nandhi may be either the strap that goes round a drum, or enmity; varatta may be either a thong or attachment; sandâna either chain or scepticism; sahanakkamam either due order or all its concomitants; paligha either obstacle or ignorance.

399. The exact meaning of balânîka is difficult to find. Does it mean, possessed of a strong army, or facing a force, or leading a force?

405. On tasa and thâvara, see Childers, s.v., and D'Alwis, Nirvâ*n*a, p. 115. On da*nd*a, 'the rod,' see Hibbert Lectures, p. 355, note.

411. Akatha*ṅ*kathi is explained by Buddhaghosa as meaning, 'free from doubt or hesitation.' He also uses katha*ṅ*kathâ in the sense of 'doubt' (verse 414). In the Kâvyâdar*s*a, III, 17, the commentator explains akatham by kathârahitam, nirvivâdam, which would mean, 'without a kathâ, a speech, a story without contradiction, unconditionally.' From our passage, however, it seems as if katha*ṅ*kathâ was a noun derived from katha*ṅ*kathayati, 'to say How, how?' so that neither the first nor the second element had anything to do with kath, 'to relate;' and in that case akatham, too, ought to be taken in the sense of 'without a Why.'

412. See verse 39. The distinction between good and evil vanishes when a

man has retired from the world, and has ceased to act, longing only for deliverance.

418. Upadhi, if not used in a technical sense, is best translated by 'passions or affections.' Technically there are four upadhis or substrata, viz. the kandhas, kâma, 'desire,' kilesa, 'sin,' and kamma, 'work.' The Brâhma*n*a may be called nirupadhi, as being free from desire, misery, and work and its consequences, but not yet of the kandhas, which end through death only. The commentator explains nirupadhi by nirupakkilesa, 'free from sin.' See Childers, s.v. nibbâna, p. 268 a.

419. Sugata is one of those many words in Buddhist literature which it is almost impossible to translate, because they have been taken in so many acceptations by the Buddhists themselves. Sugata etymologically means 'one who has fared well,' sugati means 'happiness and blessedness.' It is wrong to translate it literally by 'welcome,' for that in Sanskrit is svâgata; and we can hardly accept Dr. Eitel's statement (Handbook, p. 138) that sugata stands incorrectly for svâgata. Sugata is one of the not very numerous technical terms in Buddhism for which hitherto we know of no antecedents in earlier Brahmanism. It may have been used in the sense of 'happy and blessed,' but it never became a title, while in Buddhism it has become, not only a title, but almost a proper name of Buddha. The same applies to tathâgata, lit. 'thus come,' but used in Sanskrit very much like tathâvidha, in the sense of talis, while in Buddhism it means a Buddha. There are of course many interpretations of the word, and many reasons are given why Buddhas should be called Tathâgata (Burnouf, Introduction, p. 75, &c.). Boehtlingk s.v. supposed that, because Buddha had so many predicates, he was, for the sake of brevity, called 'such a one as he really is.' I think we may go a step further. Another word, tâd*r*isa, meaning talis, becomes in Pâli, under the form of tâdi, a name of Buddha's disciples, and afterwards of Buddha himself. If applied to Buddha's disciples, it may have meant originally 'such as he,' i.e. his fellows; but when applied to Buddha himself, it can only mean 'such a one,' i.e. 'so great a man.' The Sanskrit mârsha is probably the Pâli mâriso, which stands for mâdiso, Sk. mâd*r*isa, 'like me,' used in Pâli when a superior addresses others as his equals, and afterwards changed into a mere title of respect.

Index

The figures of this Index refer to the numbers of the verses.

Bhikkhuvagga, 360.
Bhikshu, a mendicant, 31, 32, 72, 75, 266, 267.
Bhikshu, different from Sramana and Brâhmana, 142.
Bhovâdi, arrogant, addressing venerable people by bho! 396.
Bhûri, knowledge, 282.
Bodhiruki (508–511 A.D.), 294.
Bodhyanga. See Sambodhyanga, 89.
Brahmgâlasutta, 153.
Brahman, above the gods, 230.
Brahman, with Mâra, 105.
Brâhmana, with Sramana and Bhikshu, 142.
Brâhmana, etymology of, 388.
Brâhmanavagga, 383.
Buddha's last words, 153, 154.
—commandments, 183, 185.
Buddhavagga, 179.

Convent (âvâsa), 73, 302.

Dah, to burn, not sah, 31.
Dandanidhâna, 142, 405.
Dandavagga, 129.
Death, its dominion, 86.
—king of, 170.
Dhamma, plur., forms, things, 279.
Dhammâ, plur., three of the five khandhas, vedanâ, sañña, and sankhâra, 1.
Dhammadâna, 354.
Dhammatthavagga, 256.
Dhanapâlaka, 324.
Dharma, explained, 1.
Dhâtu, eighteen, 89.
Digambaras (Gainas, followers of Mahâvîra), 141.

Dîpa, island (arhatship), 25, 26.
Dîpa, dvîpa, island, 236, 238.
Dîpankara, 236, 238.
Dîpavamsa, 21.
Disciple (sekha), 45.
Ditthi, drishti, heresy, 164.
Divyâvadâna, 141, 149.
Drinking, 247.

Eightfold, the way, 191, 273.
Elephant, Buddha, 320.

Fetters of life, 345, 346, 350.
Fire, worshipped by Brahmans, 107, 392.
Flowers, with and without scent, 51, 52.
Four truths, 190, 273.

Gandharva, 104.
Gâthâ, 101.
Gâthâsangraha, 183.
Gods, 94, 200.
Gold pieces, 186, 230 (nekkha).
Good and evil bear fruit, 119–122.
Gotama, 296.
Graha, gaha, 251.

Gainas, 104, 141.
Gambû river, gold of it, 230.
Garâvagga, 146.
Gâtaka, 9, 33, 35–39, 72, 149, 158, 179, 187, 285, 294, 306, 345.
Gatâ, sign of Saiva ascetic, 141.

Hair, platted, of Brahmans, 393, 394.
Hatred, how it ceases, 3, 4.
—ceases by love, 5.
Hitopadesa, 129.

Patricide, 294.
Piyavagga, 209.
Platted hair, 141.
Prapañka, 254.
Prasenagit, defeated by Agâtasatru, 201.
Prâtibhâna, 363.
Prâtimoksha, 183, 185.
Pravrag, 83.
Pravragita, etymology of, 388.
Proverbs, 96.
Puns, 283, 294, 295, 305.
Pupphavagga, 44.

Raga, dust, passion, 313.
Râmâyana, 129.

Sacrifice, worthless, 106.
Sahassavagga, quoted in Mahâvastu, 100.
Sahita = Tipitaka, 19.
St. Luke, 130.
St. Matthew, 252.
St. Mark, 157.
Samana, etymology of, 265.
Sâmañña, priesthood, 20.
Sambodhyanga, 89.
Samsâra, 60.
Samskâra, conception, 202.
—the five skandhas, 202.
Samyutta-nikâya, 69.
Sanatsugâtîya, 21.
Sankhâra, creature, 255.
Sankhâta, 70.
Sañgña, perception, 202.
Sâra, truth, reality, 11.
Sati, smriti, intense thought, 91.
Sayanâsanam, sayanâsanam, 185.
Self, lord of self, 160, 165.
Seven elements of knowledge, 89.

Shore, the other, 85, 384.
—the two shores, 385.
Sindhu horses, 322.
Skandha, body, 202.
Snowy mountains, 304.
Spider, 347.
Spoon, perceives no taste, 64.
Sugata, Buddha, 285, 419 (welfaring).
Sukhavagga, 197.
Suttanipâta, 20, 61, 87, 125, 141, 142, 170, 185, 205, 239, 306, 328, 339, 345, 353, 364, 375, 396–423.

Sâkala-prâtisâkhya, 352.
Sûnya, 92.
Svetambaras (Gainas, followers of Parsvanâtha), 141.

Tabernacle, maker of, 153.
Tagara, plant, 54.
Taittirîya-âranyaka, 96.
Tamhâvagga, 334.
Tathâgata, 254.
Tathâgatas, are preachers, 276.
Ten evil states, 137.
Thirty-six passions, 339.
Thought, word, and deed, 96.
Thoughts, their influence, 1.
Tirthankara, 104.
Tonsure, 264.
Trisarana, 190.
Trividhadvâra, thought, word, and deed, 96.
Twin-verses, 1.

Ukkutika, see Utkatukâsana, 141.
Uncreated (akata), 97.
Upâdâna, 20.
Upadhi, 418.
Upadhiviveka, 203.

Upamâ, aupamya, 129.
Upasarga, misfortune, 139.
Ûrdhvamsrotas, 218.
Utka*t*ukâsana, sitting on the hams,
   141.

Vâha, horse, or vaha, wave, 339.
Vana, forest and lust, 283.
Vasish*t*ha-Bharadvâ*g*a-sûtra, 396.
Vassikâ flower, 377.
Vassikî, flower, 55.
Vedanâ, sensation, 202.
Videha, king of, 200.
Vi*g*ñâna, knowledge, 202.
Vimoksha, freedom, 92, 93.

Vinaya-pi*t*aka, 28, 307.
Vish*n*u-sûtra, 9.
Vi*s*vabhû Tathâgata, 49.
Viveka, separation, retirement, 75, 87.

Works, good, 220.
World, the next, 176.
—of the gods, 177.

Yama, 44, 45, 235.
Yama's messengers, 235.
Yamakavagga, 1.
Ye dhammâ, &c., 183.
Yellow dress, 9, 10, 307.
Yoni*s*ah, truly, thoroughly, 326.

Endnotes

Introduction to the Dhammapada

1. See Feer, Journal Asiatique, 1871, p. 263. There is now at least one complete MS. of the Tipitaka, the Phayre MS., at the India Office, and Professor Forchhammer has just published a most useful List of Pâli MSS., collected in Burma, the largest collection hitherto known.

2. See Childers, s.v. Nikâya, and extracts from Buddhaghosa's commentary on the Brahmagâla-sutta.

3. The figures within brackets refer to the other list of books in the Khuddaka-nikâya. See also p. xxxv.

4. M. Léon Feer in the Journal Asiatique, 1871, p. 266, mentions another commentary of a more philosophical character, equally ascribed to Buddhaghosa, and having the title Vivara Bra Dhammapada, i.e. L'auguste Dhammapada dévoilé. Professor Forchhammer in his 'List of Manuscripts,' 1879-80, mentions the following works in connection with the Dhammapada: Dhammapada-Nissayo; Dh. P. Atthakathâ by Buddhaghosa; Dh. P. Atthakathâ Nissayo, 3 vols., containing a complete translation of the commentary; Dh. P. Vatthu. Of printed books he quotes: Kayanupassanakyam, a work based on the Garâvaggo, Mandalay, 1876 (390 pages), and Dhammapada-desanakyam, printed in 'British Burma News.'

5. Indian Antiquary, 1880, p. 233.

6. See some important remarks on this subject in Fausböll's Introduction to Sutta-nipâta, p. xi.
7. Bigandet, Life of Gaudama (Rangoon, 1866), p. 350; but also p. 120 note.
8. See Childers, s.v. Tipiṭaka. There is a curious passage in Buddhaghosa's account of the First Council. 'Now one may ask,' he says, 'Is there or is there not in this first Parâgika anything to be taken away or added?' I reply, There is nothing in the words of the Blessed Buddha that can be taken away, for the Buddhas speak not even a single syllable in vain, yet in the words of disciples and devatâs there are things which may be omitted, and these the elders who made the recension, did omit. On the other hand, additions are everywhere necessary, and accordingly, whenever it was necessary to add anything, they added it. If it be asked, What are the additions referred to? I reply, Only sentences necessary to connect the text, as 'at that time,' 'again at that time,' 'and so forth.'
9. Pèlerins Bouddhistes, vol. i, p. 158.
10. Mahâvaṃsa, p. 37; Dîpavaṃsa VII, 28–31; Buddhaghosha's Parables, p. xviii.
11. Bigandet, Life of Gaudama, p. 351.
12. Dr. E. Müller (Indian Antiquary, Nov. 1880, p. 270) has discovered inscriptions in Ceylon, belonging to Devanapiya Maharâga Gâminī Tissa, whom he identifies with Vaṭṭagâmani.
13. The same account is given in the Dîpavaṃsa XX, 20, and in the Sârasaṅgraha, as quoted by Spence Hardy, Legends, p. 192. As throwing light on the completeness of the Buddhist canon at the time of King Vaṭṭagâmani, it should be mentioned that, according to the commentary on the Mahâvaṃsa (Turnour, p. liii), the sect of the Dhammarukikas established itself at the Abhayavihâra, which had been constructed by Vaṭṭagâmani, and that one of the grounds of their secession was their refusing to acknowledge the Parivâra (thus I read instead of Pariwána) as part of the Vinaya-piṭaka. According to the Dîpavaṃsa (VII, 42) Mahinda knew the Parivâra.
14. A note is added, stating that several portions of the other two divisions also of the Piṭakattaya were translated into the Sinhalese language, and that these alone are consulted by the priests, who are unacquainted with Pâli. On the other hand, it is stated that the Sinhalese text of the Aṭṭhakathâ exists no longer. See Spence Hardy, Legends, p. xxv, and p. 69.
15. 'Ungefähr 50 Jahre älter als Mahânâma ist Buddhaghosha,' see Westergaard, Über Buddha's Todesjahr, p. 99.
16. Introduction, p. ii. The Kûlavaṃsa is mentioned with the Mahâvaṃsa, both as the works of Mahânâma, by Professor Forchhammer in his List of Pâli MSS.
17. Introduction, p. xci.
18. See Rhys Davids, Journal of the Royal Asiatic Society, 1875, p. 196.

19. Introduction, p. liii.

20. Mr. Turnour added a note in which he states that Dîpavaṃsa is here meant for Mahâvaṃsa, but whether brought down to this period, or only to the end of the reign of Mahâsena, to which alone the Tîkâ extends, there is no means of ascertaining (p. 257).

21. Dr. Oldenberg informs me that the commentator quotes various readings in the text of the Mahâvaṃsa.

22. The passage, quoted by Professor Minayeff from the Sâsanavaṃsa, would assign to Buddhaghosa the date of 930 − 543 = 387 A.D., which can easily be reconciled with his accepted date. If he is called the contemporary of Siripâla, we ought to know who that Siripâla is.

23. See Bigandet, Life of Gaudama, pp. 351, 381.

24. On this vihâra, its foundation and character, see Oldenberg, Vinaya, vol. i, p. liii; Hiouen-thsang, III, p. 487 seq.

25. Mahâvaṃsa, p. 250, translated by Turnour.

26. The Burmese entertain the highest respect for Buddhaghosa. Bishop Bigandet, in his Life or Legend of Gaudama (Rangoon, 1866), writes: 'It is perhaps as well to mention here an epoch which has been, at all times, famous in the history of Budhism in Burma. I allude to the voyage which a Religious of Thaton, named Budhagosa, made to Ceylon, in the year of religion 943 = 400 A.D. The object of this voyage was to secure a copy of the scriptures. He succeeded in his undertaking. He made use of the Burmese, or rather Talaing characters, in transcribing the manuscripts, which were written with the characters of Magatha. The Burmans lay much stress upon that voyage, and always carefully note down the year it took place. In fact, it is to Budhagosa that the people living on the shores of the Gulf of Martaban owe the possession of the Budhist scriptures. From Thaton, the collection made by Budhagosa was transferred to Pagan, six hundred and fifty years after it had been imported from Ceylon.' See ibid. p. 392.

27. He had written the Ñânodaya, and the Aṭṭhasâlinî, a commentary on the Dhamma-saṅgaṇi, before he went to Ceylon. Cf. Mahâvaṃsa, p. 251.

28. He learnt the five Nikâyas, and the seven sections (of the Abhidhamma); the two Vibhaṅgas of the Vinaya, the Parivâra and the Khandhaka. See Dîpavaṃsa VII, 42.

29. On the importance of oral tradition in the history of Sanskrit literature see the writer's Ancient Sanskrit Literature, 1859, pp. 497–524.

30. Mahâvaṃsa, p. 207; Dîpavaṃsa XX, 20.

31. Mahâvaṃsa, p. 251.

32. See Childers, s.v. Nikâya.

33. Dîpavaṃsa VII, 40.

34. Dîpavamsa VII, 55.
35. Dr. Oldenberg, in his Introduction to the Vinaya-pitaka, p. xxxii.
36. Oldenberg, Vinaya-pitaka I, p. xvi, treats it as an extended reading of the Pâtimokkha.
37. The Mahâparinibbâna-sutta, ed. by Childers, Journal of the Royal Asiatic Society, translated with other Suttas by Rhys Davids (S. B. E. vol. xi). Sept Suttas Palis, par Grimblot, Paris, 1876.
38. The first four are sometimes called the Four Nikâyas, the five together the Five Nikâyas. They represent the Dharma, as settled at the First and Second Councils, described in the Kullavagga (Oldenberg, I, p. xi).
39. Sometimes Khuddaka-nikâya stands for the whole Vinaya and Abhidhammapitaka, with the fifteen divisions here given of Khuddaka-nikâya. In the commentary on the Brahmagâla-sutta it is said that the Dîghanikâya professors rehearsed the text of the Gâtaka, Mahâ and Kulla Niddesa, Patisambhidâmagga, Suttanipâta, Dhammapada, Udâna, Itivuttaka, Vimâna, and Petavatthu, Thera and Therî Gâthâ, and called it Khuddakagantha, and made it a canonical text, forming part of the Abhidhamma; while the Magghimanikâya professors assert that, with the addition of the Kariyâpitaka, Apadâna, and Buddhavamsa, the whole of this Khuddakagantha was included in the Suttapitaka. See Childers, s.v. Nikâya. See also p. xviii.
40. Published by Childers, Journal of the Royal Asiatic Society, 1869.
41. Published by Fausböll, 1855.
42. Thirty translated by Sir Coomâra Swâmy; the whole by Fausböll, in Sacred Books of the East, vol. x.
43. Published by Fausböll, translated by Rhys Davids.
44. Buddhaghosa does not say whether these were recited at the First Council.
45. Partly translated by Gogerly, Journal of the Asiatic Society of Ceylon, 1852.
46. Cf. Gogerly, Journal of the Asiatic Society of Ceylon, 1848, p. 7.
47. See Oldenberg's Vinaya-pitaka, Introduction, p. xxv. The kings Agâtasatru (485–453 B.C.), Udâyin (453–437 B.C.), and Munda (437–429 B.C.) are all mentioned in the Tipitaka. See Oldenberg, Zeitschrift der D. M. G., XXXIV, pp. 752, 753.
48. Oldenberg, Introduction, p. xxix.
49. Oldenberg, loc. cit. p. xx.
50. Loc. cit. pp. xxvi–xxviii.
51. There are several Chinese translations of Sûtras on the subject of the Mahâparinirvâna. Three belong to the Mahâyâna school: 1. Mahâparinirvâna-sûtra, translated by Dharmaraksha, about 414–423 A.D.; afterwards revised, 424–453 (Nos. 113, 114). 2. Translation by Fa-hian and Buddhabhadra, about 415 A.D.; less complete (No. 120). 3. Translation (vaipnlya) by Dharmarak-

sha I, i.e. *Ku* Fa-hu, about 261–308 A.D. (No. 116). Three belong to the Hînayâna school: 1. Mahâparinirvâna-sûtra, translated by Po-fa-tsu, about 290–306 A.D. (No. 552). 2. Translation under the Eastern Tsin dynasty, 317–420 A.D. (No. 119). 3. Translation by Fa-hian, about 415 A.D. (No. 118).

52. Feer, Revue Critique, 1870, No. 24, p. 377.

53. Introduction, pp. x, xii.

54. Dr. Oldenberg informs me that pi*t*aka occurs in the *Kan*kîsuttanta in the Ma*ggh*ima Nikâya (Turnour's MS., fol. the), but applied to the Veda. He also refers to the tipi*t*akâkâryas mentioned in the Western Cave inscriptions as compared with the Pa*ñ*kanekâyâka in the square A*s*oka character inscriptions (Cunningham, Bharhut, pl. lvi, No. 52). In the Sûtrak*r*id-an*g*a of the *G*ainas, too, the term pi*d*aga*m* occurs (MS. Berol. fol. 77 a). He admits, however, that pi*t*aka or tipi*t*aka, as the technical name of the Buddhist canon, has not yet been met with in that canon itself, and defends Dvipi-*t*aka only as a convenient term.

55. See Academy, August 28, 1880, Division of Buddhist Scriptures.

56. Oldenberg, Introduction, p. xii; Turnour, Journal of the Asiatic Society of Bengal, vi, p. 510 seq.

57. Mahâva*m*sa, p. 21.

58. According to Bigandet, Life of Gaudama, p. 361, the era of Buddha's death was introduced by A*g*âta*s*atru, at the conclusion of the First Council, and began in the year 146 of the older Eetzana era (p. 12). See, however, Rhys Davids, Num. Orient. vi, p. 38. In the Kâra*n*da-vyûha, p. 96, a date is given as 300 after the Nirvâna, 'triti*y*e varsha*s*a*t*e gate mama parinir*v*ritasya' In the A*s*oka-avadâna we read, mama nir*v*ritim ârabhya *s*atavarshagata Upagupto nâma bhikshur utpatsyati.

59. Über Buddha's Todesjahr (1860), 1862.

60. The Greek name Sandrokyptus shows that the Pâli corruption *K*andagutta was not yet the recognised name of the king.

61. Mr. Rhys Davids accepts 315 B.C. as the date when, after the murder of king Nanda, *K*andragupta stept into the vacant throne, though he had begun to count his reign seven or eight years before. Buddhism, p. 220.

62. Westergaard, loc. cit. p. 128.

63. Jaartelling der Zuidelijke Buddhisten, 1873.

64. See Professor Kern's remark in Indian Antiquary, 1874, p. 79.

65. When Professor Kern states that the Mahâva*m*sa (p. 32) places the Third Council 218 years after Buddha's death, this is not so. A*s*oka's abhisheka takes place in that year. The prophecy that a calamity would befall their religion, 118 years after the Second Council (Mahâva*m*sa, p. 28), does not refer to the Council, but to *K*andâsoka's accession, 477 − 218 = 259 B.C.

66. Westergaard, 320–296; Kern, 323–298.
67. Three New Edicts of Asoka, Bombay, 1877; Second Notice, Bombay, 1878.
68. Mr. Rhys Davids on p. 50 assigns the 25 years of Bindusâra rightly to the Purânas, the 28 years to the Ceylon Chronicles.
69. Three Edicts, p. 21; Second Notice, pp. 9, 10.
70. See Jacobi, Kalpa-sûtra of Bhadrabâhu, and Oldenberg, Zeitschrift der D. M. G., XXXIV, p. 749.
71. Oldenberg, loc. cit. p. 750.
72. The Dîpavamsa, an ancient Buddhist historical record. London, 1879.
73. Assuming twenty to be the minimum age at which a man could be ordained.
74. I take 60 (80), as given in Dîpavamsa V, 95, 107, instead of 66 (86), as given in Dîpavamsa V, 94.
75. The combined patriarchates of Saunaka and Siggava are given as 99 by the Dîpavamsa.
76. Cf. Dhammâpada, v. 385, nibbânam sugatena desitam.
77. Buddhist Nirvâna, p. 62.
78. Revue Critique, 1870, p. 378.
79. D'Alwis, Pâli Grammar, p. 61.
80. See M. M.'s Sanskrit Grammar, § 519.
81. Mr. D'Alwis' arguments (Buddhist Nirvâna, pp. 63–67) in support of this view, viz. the dhammapada may be a collective term, do not seem to me to strengthen my own conjecture.
82. Dhammapada from Chinese, p. 4.
83. Spence Hardy, Manual, p. 496.
84. Burnouf, Lotus, p. 520, 'Ajoutons, pour terminer ce que nous trouvons à dire sur le mot magga, quelque commentaire qu'on en donne d'ailleurs, que suivant une définition rapportée par Turnour, le magga renferme une sous-division que l'on nomme patipadâ, en sanscrit pratipad. Le magga, dit Turnour, est la voie qui conduit au Nibbâna, la patipadâ, littéralement "la marche pas à pas, ou le degré," est la vie de rectitude qu'on doit suivre, quand on marche dans la voie du magga.'
85. See Spence Hardy, Manual, p. 496. Should not katurvidha-dharmapada, mentioned on p. 497, be translated by 'the fourfold path of the Law'? It can hardly be the fourfold word of the Law.
86. Catena, p. 207.
87. 'Several of the chapters have been translated by Mr. Gogerly, and have appeared in The Friend, vol. iv, 1840.' (Spence Hardy, Eastern Monachism, p. 169.)
88. Buddhaghosha's Parables, translated from Burmese by Captain T. Rogers,

R.E. With an Introduction, containing Buddha's Dhammapada, translated from Pâli by F. Max Müller. London, 1870.

89. Le Dhammapada avec introduction et notes par Fernand Hû, suivi du Sutra en 42 articles, traduit du Tibetain, par Léon Feer. Paris, 1878.

90. Texts from the Buddhist Canon, commonly known as Dhammapada, translated from the Chinese by Samuel Beal. London, 1878.

91. Beal, Dhammapada, p. 30. The real number of verses, however, is 760. In the Pâli text, too, there are five verses more than stated in the Index; see M. M., Buddhaghosha's Parables, p. ix, note; Beal, loc. cit. p. 11, note.

92. Introduction to Buddhaghosha's Parables, 1870, p. 1.

93. See Lassen, Indische Alterthumskunde, vol. ii, p. 700, note. That Lassen is right in taking the Σαρμᾶναι, mentioned by Megasthenes, for Brahmanic, not for Buddhist ascetics, might be proved also by their dress. Dresses made of the bark of trees are not strictly Buddhistic.

94. See Dhammapada, v. 388; Bastian, Völker des östlichen Asien, vol. iii, p. 412: 'Ein buddhistischer Mönch erklärte mir, dass die Brahmanen ihren Namen führten, als Lente, die ihre Sünden abgespült hätten.' See also Lalitavistara, p. 551, line 1; p. 553, line 7.

2: On Earnestness

1. There is nothing in the tenth section of the Dhammapada, as translated by Beal, corresponding to the verses of this chapter.

4: Flowers

1. See Beal, Dhammapada, p. 75.

About the Translator

F. Max Müller was a German-born philologist. He studied and worked in the United Kingdom for the majority of his life and became one of the foremost Western academic scholars interested in India and comparative religions.

THE ESSENTIAL WISDOM LIBRARY

Sacred Texts for Modern Readers

ST. FRANCIS OF ASSISI

THE TAO TE CHING OF LAO TZU

THE BHAGAVAD GITA

EDWARD VILJOEN

THE I CHING OR BOOK OF CHANGES

BRIAN BROWNE WALKER

BUDDHISM

JUAN GONZÁLEZ OLIVER

THE KEBRA NAGAST

EDITED BY GERALD HAUSMAN

THE TOLTEC WAY

SUSAN GREGG

THE KYBALION

THREE INITIATES

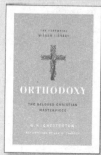

ORTHODOXY

THE BELOVED CHRISTIAN MASTERPIECE

G. K. CHESTERTON

THE DHAMMAPADA

F. MAX MÜLLER

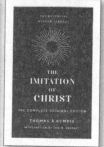

THE IMITATION OF CHRIST

THE COMPLETE ORIGINAL EDITION

THOMAS À KEMPIS

INTERIOR CASTLE

THE COMPLETE ORIGINAL EDITION

ST. TERESA OF AVILA

APRIL 2023   **AUGUST 2023**

ST. MARTIN'S ESSENTIALS